Workbook

Hospitality Services

Food & Lodging

Linda G. Smock, M.S.
Family and Consumer Sciences
Consultant and Writer
Largo, Florida

Hospitality Services: Food & Lodging Text
Johnny Sue Reynolds, Ph.D., CFCS

Publisher
The Goodheart-Willcox Company, Inc.
Tinley Park, Illinois

Contents

Part 3 The Lodging Industry

Part 4 The Business of Hospitality

The World of Hospitality

Kick Off!

Activity A   Name _____

Chapter 1   Date _____ Period _____

Part 1

Read each statement below. Do you agree with the statement? Write *yes* or *no* in the *Agree?* column. Be ready to explain your reasons for each answer.

Statement	Agree?	Text Supports?
1. Hospitality means meeting the needs of guests with kindness and goodwill.		
2. The hospitality industry refers to providing services to people in your home.		
3. The hospitality industry has no impact on the economy of a country.		
4. Hospitality workers may be as diverse as the customers they serve.		
5. The hospitality industry is a complex business.		
6. The lodging industry includes hotels, campgrounds, and airports.		

(continued)

Statement	Agree?	Text Supports?
7. Recreation businesses provide activities for rest, relaxation, and enjoyment.		
8. Business travel usually centers around rest, relaxation, and enjoyment.		
9. Chains and franchises are examples of single-unit businesses.		
10. Two examples of career and technical student organizations (CTSOs) for students interested in hospitality are FCCLA and SkillsUSA.		

Part 2

Look in the text to find support for each statement. If the text supports a statement, write *yes* in the *Text Supports?* column. Then write the text page number in the space below the statement. If the text does not support the statement, write *no* in the *Text Supports?* column. Then, in the space below the statement, rewrite the statement so that it is supported by the text.

Hospitality Terms Chapter 1

Name _____

Date _____ Period _____

Part 1

Match each term below to its definition. Write the term in the blank in front of its definition.

_____ 1. A business that has more than one location under the same name and the same ownership.

_____ 2. A period of time during which a person rests and is free from daily obligations.

_____ 3. A business that has only one location and one unit.

_____ 4. A group of people who have organized themselves to improve themselves, their profession, and their industry.

_____ 5. A trip that includes several segments of the hospitality industry at one fee.

_____ 6. A name, logo, tagline, or any combination of these that distinguishes a product from its competitors.

_____ 7. A place to sleep for one or more nights.

_____ 8. Activities that people do for rest, relaxation, and enjoyment.

_____ 9. Businesses that prepare food for customers.

_____ 10. Meeting the needs of guests with kindness and goodwill.

_____ 11. Businesses that physically move people from one place to another.

_____ 12. Travel that is done as part of a person's job.

_____ 13. Travel that is done for rest and relaxation.

_____ 14. An organization for students with an interest in a career area.

brand

business travel

career and technical student organization

chain

food and beverage industry

hospitality

lodging

package

pleasure travel

professional association

recreation

single-unit business

travel industry

vacation

(continued)

Part 2

Match each term below to its definition. Write the term in the blank in front of its definition.

_____ 15. Services that are provided to people who are away from home.

_____ 16. Businesses that prepare food for customers.

_____ 17. A place to sleep.

_____ 18. Businesses that provide overnight accommodations.

_____ 19. Businesses that provide activities for rest, relaxation, and enjoyment.

_____ 20. Businesses that organize and promote travel and vacations.

_____ 21. Travel done for rest and relaxation.

_____ 22. A business that has more than one unit or more than one location.

_____ 23. The right to do business using the brand and products of another business.

_____ 24. The person who buys the right to use the brand and products of another business.

_____ 25. The person who owns a chain and sells franchises.

_____ 26. The legal document that sets up a franchise.

_____ 27. The money paid by the franchisee to the franchisor for the franchise.

_____ 28. Another name for a single-unit business.

_____ 29. A business that provides overnight accommodations.

accommodation

foodservice industry

franchise

franchise agreement

franchisee

franchise fee

franchisor

hospitality industry

independent business

leisure travel

lodging industry

lodging property

multiple-unit business

recreation industry

tourism industry

(continued)

Part 3

A *synonym* is a word or term that has the same meaning as another word or term. In the space before each term below, write a synonym.

_____ 30. chain

_____ 31. foodservice industry

_____ 32. hospitality industry

_____ 33. leisure travel

_____ 34. lodging

_____ 35. professional association

_____ 36. single-unit business

_____ 37. travel industry

Business Structures

Name _____

Date _____ Period _____

Respond to the statements or questions by writing an answer in the space below each one.

1. Describe the two basic types of business structures, and give an example of each that is available in your community.

   single-unit business: _____

   _____

   multiple-unit business: _____

   _____

2. Describe the two types of multiple business structures, and give an example of each that is available in your local community.

   chain: _____

   _____

   franchise: _____

   _____

3. Describe the difference between a franchisor and a franchisee. _____

   _____

   _____

4. Explain the purpose of a franchise agreement and the franchise fee. _____

   _____

   _____

5. Give an example of each of the following in your community or in a nearby town. You may use a phone book to assist you.

   hotel chain: _____

   restaurant chain: _____

   campground chain: _____

   independent restaurant: _____

   chain recreation facility: _____

6. Explain in your own words the difference in a franchise and a chain.

   _____

   _____

   _____

   _____

   _____

Revisiting Chapter 1

Name _____

Date _____ Period _____

Respond to the statements or questions by writing an answer in the space provided.

1. Name the world's largest industry. _____

2. What is the major thing the hospitality industry puts into a nation's economy? _____

_____

3. List three factors that make hospitality businesses diverse. _____

_____

_____

4. List three factors that make the people who work in hospitality diverse. _____

_____

_____

5. The hospitality industry is complex because it consists of four segments. Complete the chart below. In each row, name one of the segments in Column A, write a description of the segment in Column B, and give one example of the segment in Column C.

A. Segment	B. Description	C. Example

6. List the two reasons that people travel. _____

_____

7. A family takes a vacation to a national park. This is an example of what type of travel?

_____

8. A businesswoman travels to another country to meet with clients. This is an example of what type of travel? _____

_____

9. Why must the four segments of the hospitality industry work together? _____

_____

_____

(continued)

10. List the two basic structures of business. _____

_____

11. Paul Fong owns six Chinese restaurants. What is the structure of his business? _____

_____

12. Betsy Harrington owns a bed-and-breakfast. It is not part of any other business. What is the structure of this business? _____

_____

13. Why does a business develop a brand? _____

_____

_____

_____

_____

14. The term *franchise* refers to two related things. Name them. _____

_____

_____

15. Name the term used for the person who owns a chain and sells a franchise to another person.

_____

16. Name the term used for a person who buys a franchise. _____

_____

17. What is the term for a group of people who belong to the same profession and organize themselves to work to improve themselves, their profession, and their industry? _____

_____

18. List three things that professional associations do. _____

_____

_____

19. List three advantages of belonging to a professional association. _____

_____

_____

20. What kind of organization can students join if they want to get involved with professional development? Give one example of such an organization.

_____

_____

_____

_____

_____

Service: The Heart of Hospitality

Kick Off!

Activity A	Name _____
Chapter 2	Date _____ Period _____

Part 1

Read each statement below. Do you agree with the statement? Write *yes* or *no* in the *Agree?* column. Be ready to explain your reasons for each answer.

Statement	Agree?	Text Supports?
1. Customers are not important to a hospitality business.		
2. The words *guest* and *customer* have the same meaning.		
3. Psychological needs must be met before physical needs can be met.		
4. Hospitality workers should be concerned about the expectations of customers.		
5. A server is one example of a back-of-the-house employee.		
6. An employee who slouches makes a good impression on guests.		

(continued)

Statement	Agree?	Text Supports?
7. A clean, attractive entrance makes a good impression on guests.		
8. All guests hate to wait, so there's no need to be nice to them when they have to wait.		
9. Hospitality workers should never address customers by name.		
10. When a customer complains, it's okay to just blame someone else.		

Part 2

Look in the text to find support for each statement. If the text supports a statement, write *yes* in the *Text Supports?* column. Then write the text page number in the space below the statement. If the text does not support the statement, write *no* in the *Text Supports?* column. Then, in the space below the statement, rewrite the statement so that it is supported by the text.

Hospitality Terms Chapter 2

Name _____

Date _____ Period _____

Part 1

Match each term below to its definition. Write the term in the blank in front of its definition.

_____ 1. An activity that is done for another person.

_____ 2. Total customer experience with a business.

_____ 3. Service that meets or exceeds what the customer expects.

_____ 4. The positive feelings customers have about a business that meets their needs.

_____ 5. Providing the same good service and products to customers each and every time they come to a business.

_____ 6. Someone who purchases products or services from a hospitality business.

_____ 7. The area in a hospitality business that guests usually do not see.

_____ 8. The area in a hospitality business that guests usually see.

back-of-the-house

consistent quality service

customer satisfaction

customer service

front-of-the-house

guest

quality service

service

service experience

(continued)

Part 2

Match each term below to its definition. Write the term in the blank in front of its definition.

_____ 9. Informal conversation people have about their experiences with a business.

_____ 10. Employees whose main function is to interact with customers.

_____ 11. A time when the customer's experience makes a bigger impact on customer satisfaction than at other times.

_____ 12. Employees whose work rarely involves interacting with customers.

_____ 13. An interaction between a customer and a staff member.

_____ 14. Someone who purchases services or products from a business.

_____ 15. An employee who can anticipate customer needs.

_____ 16. Ability to know how another person feels.

back-of-the-house employees

critical moment

customer

customer complaints

customer-focused employee

empathy

front-of-the-house employees

service encounter

word-of-mouth publicity

Hospitality Employees

Activity C

Name _____

Chapter 2

Date _____ Period _____

Part 1

The purpose of the chart below is to clarify the differences between front-of-the-house and back-of-the-house employees. Complete the chart by filling in Columns A and B.

	A. Front-of-the-house	B. Back-of-the-house
1. interaction with customers		
2. interaction with other employees		
3. duties and responsibilities		

Part 2

For each hospitality employee below, decide whether that employee works in the front-of-the-house or back-of-the-house. Place an *F* in the blank to identify front-of-the house-employees and a *B* in the blank to identify back-of-the-house employees.

_____ 4. accounting staff

_____ 5. banquet server

_____ 6. bartender

_____ 7. bell attendant

_____ 8. busser

_____ 9. cashier

_____ 10. chef

_____ 11. concierge

_____ 12. cook

_____ 13. dishwasher

_____ 14. door attendant

_____ 15. engineering staff

_____ 16. executive housekeeper

_____ 17. food preparation staff

_____ 18. front desk agent

_____ 19. host or hostess

_____ 20. housekeeper

_____ 21. human resources staff

_____ 22. laundry attendant

_____ 23. marketing staff

_____ 24. parking attendant

_____ 25. receiving clerk

_____ 26. reservations agent

_____ 27. room attendant

_____ 28. sales staff

_____ 29. security officer

_____ 30. server

_____ 31. setup staff

_____ 32. steward

Revisiting Chapter 2

Name _____

Date _____ Period _____

Choose from the words listed below to complete each sentence below. Write the correct word in the blank in front of the sentence it completes.

complaints	focused	needs
communication	guest	posture
consistent	impression	publicity
contact	laundry	quality
customers	lobby	response
empathy	moment	service
encounters	name	smile

_____ 1. The main reason for the hospitality business is to serve its _____.

_____ 2. The words *customer* and _____ are sometimes used interchangeably in the hospitality industry.

_____ 3. Addressing a customer by _____ can help meet his or her acceptance and esteem needs.

_____ 4. Customer satisfaction is directly related to the _____ of the service provided by the business.

_____ 5. Understanding that customers may feel tired after traveling is an example of _____.

_____ 6. With _____ quality service, customers are assured they will receive the same level of service each time they visit the business.

_____ 7. A customer-_____ employee can anticipate his or her customers' needs.

_____ 8. Quality service depends on positive service _____.

_____ 9. A _____ is part of the uniform for all hospitality employees.

_____ 10. A quick _____ to a customer's request shows the employee's competency, concern for the customer, and willingness to help.

_____ 11. Resolving an upset customer's _____ is key to regaining the customer's loyalty to the business.

_____ 12. Employees at every level of the hospitality industry must have good _____ skills.

_____ 13. When customers discuss with other people the service they received at a hospitality business, this is known as word-of-mouth _____.

(continued)

_____ 14. In a hotel, the _____ is an example of the front-of-the-house.

_____ 15. In a hotel, the _____ is an example of the back-of-the-house.

_____ 16. All employees are responsible for making sure that customers receive the best _____ possible.

_____ 17. Immediate eye _____ communicates that a customer's needs are important enough for you to devote your undivided attention.

_____ 18. A worker with good _____ holds his or her head up, back straight, and shoulders back.

_____ 19. Guests who call ahead often form a first _____ of the business based on the service they received during the phone call.

_____ 20. A critical _____ is a time when the customer's experience makes a bigger impact on customer satisfaction than at other times.

Hospitality Past, Present, and Future

Kick Off!

Activity A	Name _____
Chapter 3	Date _____ Period _____

Part 1

Read each statement below. Write *yes* or *no* in the *Agree?* column. Be ready to explain your reasons for each answer.

Statement	Agree?	Text Supports?
1. Three countries played an important role in the early history of the hospitality industry. They are England, the United States, and Italy.		
2. The hospitality industry changed as the methods of transportation changed.		
3. Grand hotels began in Europe.		
4. Commercial airlines had little effect on the hospitality industry.		
5. Diversity of the workforce has changed the American hospitality industry.		
6. The Americans with Disabilities Act was passed to insure that people with disabilities are treated fairly.		

(continued)

Statement	Agree?	Text Supports?
7. Demand for hospitality services varies with the seasons.		
8. Weather has little or no effect on the hospitality industry.		
9. The global economy consists of the interconnected economies of the Western nations.		
10. Because the future cannot be accurately predicted, consumer research is worthless.		

Part 2

Look in the text to find support for each statement. If the text supports a statement, write *yes* in the *Text Supports?* column. Then write the text page number in the space below the statement. If the text does not support the statement, write *no* in the *Text Supports?* column. Then, in the space below the statement, rewrite the statement so that it is supported by the text.

Hospitality Terms Chapter 3

Name _____

Date _____ Period _____

For each term in this chapter, develop a term overview. This term overview consists of the following three parts: a. your own definition, b. the textbook definition, and c. a sentence using the term. The first one is done for you.

1. souvenir

    a. Define the term in your own words.

    Something that you buy when you travel to remember the place you visited.

    b. Write the definition from the textbook.

    An item that reminds you of a place you visited

    c. Write a sentence using the term.

    As we traveled along the interstate, we noticed many places where we could stop to buy souvenirs.

2. hotelier

    a. Define the term in your own words.

    _____

    _____

    b. Write the definition from the textbook.

    _____

    _____

    c. Write a sentence using the term.

    _____

    _____

3. motel

    a. Define the term in your own words.

    _____

    _____

    b. Write the definition from the textbook.

    _____

    _____

    c. Write a sentence using the term.

    _____

    _____

(continued)

4. amenity

   a. Define the term in your own words.

   _____

   _____

   b. Write the definition from the textbook.

   _____

   _____

   c. Write a sentence using the term.

   _____

   _____

5. diversity

   a. Define the term in your own words.

   _____

   _____

   b. Write the definition from the textbook.

   _____

   _____

   c. Write a sentence using the term.

   _____

   _____

6. accessible

   a. Define the term in your own words.

   _____

   _____

   b. Write the definition from the textbook.

   _____

   _____

   c. Write a sentence using the term.

   _____

   _____

7. peak seasons

   a. Define the term in your own words.

   _____

   _____

(continued)

b. Write the definition from the textbook.

_____

_____

c. Write a sentence using the term.

_____

_____

8. off-peak seasons
   a. Define the term in your own words.

_____

_____

   b. Write the definition from the textbook.

_____

_____

   c. Write a sentence using the term.

_____

_____

9. recession
   a. Define the term in your own words.

_____

_____

   b. Write the definition from the textbook.

_____

_____

   c. Write a sentence using the term.

_____

_____

10. expansion
    a. Define the term in your own words.

_____

_____

    b. Write the definition from the textbook.

_____

_____

(continued)

c. Write a sentence using the term.

_____

_____

11. globalization

a. Define the term in your own words.

_____

_____

b. Write the definition from the textbook.

_____

_____

c. Write a sentence using the term.

_____

_____

12. global economy

a. Define the term in your own words.

_____

_____

b. Write the definition from the textbook.

_____

_____

c. Write a sentence using the term.

_____

_____

13. transnational corporation

a. Define the term in your own words.

_____

_____

b. Write the definition from the textbook.

_____

_____

c. Write a sentence using the term.

_____

_____

Hospitality Trends

Activity C

Chapter 3

Name _____

Date _____ Period _____

Four general types of trends affect all kinds of businesses, including hospitality businesses:

demographic trends: changes in the size of a group of people

social trends: changes in the structure or beliefs of society

lifestyle trends: changes in the way people live their lives

technology trends: changes in technology

Column A in the chart below lists several trends. For each trend, name the type of trend it is in Column B. In Column C, describe a product or service that a hospitality business might develop for this trend.

A. Trend	B. Type	C. Product or service
1. More businesswomen are traveling.		
2. More families are eating at restaurants.		
3. Travelers want to be able to exercise.		
4. Gaming has become socially acceptable.		
5. It is possible to make safe, secure reservations on the Internet.		
6. Drinking specialty coffee is very popular.		
7. The number of people older than 65 is increasing.		
8. People are taking many short weekend vacations instead of one long vacation.		
9. People want to take ready-to-eat foods home for dinner.		
10. Travelers are taking their laptops with them, and they want to connect to the Internet.		

Revisiting Chapter 3

Activity D   Name _____

Chapter 3   Date _____ Period _____

Read each statement below. Fill in the letters for the missing words. Then either complete the statement or answer the question.

1. The three c _ _ _ _ _ _ _ _ that played an important role in the history of hospitality are
   _____.

2. In the 1600s in the United States, travelers ate and slept in the inns along
   s _ _ _ _ _ _ _ _ _ routes. The major reason for stopping was so that drivers could
   _____

3. The development of travel by r _ _ _ _ _ _ _ had a big impact on the hospitality industry. What type of hotel was built to meet the needs of these travelers? _____
   _____

4. At the same time, a new hospitality profession began: h _ _ _ _ _ _ _. What does this
   professional do? _____

5. A m _ _ _ _ combines the services of a hotel with the convenience needed by someone traveling by car. Parking is _____

6. As air travel became more common, many hospitality businesses were developed at
   a _ _ _ _ _ _ _. Name two types of hospitality businesses developed at these locations.
   _____

7. Guests must receive the same good s _ _ _ _ _ _ every time they come to a business. How
   do managers make sure this happens? _____

8. The hospitality workforce is d _ _ _ _ _ _ _ because the people who work in hospitality
   have a variety of _____

9. The A _ _ _ _ _ _ _ _ _ with D _ _ _ _ _ _ _ _ _ _ _ _ _ Act was created to make
   sure people with disabilities are treated fairly. One of the requirements of this Act is _____
   _____

10. P _ _ _ s _ _ _ _ _ _ _ are those seasons with the h _ _ _ _ _ _ demand. Those
    seasons with the lowest demands are known as _____
    _____

11. The w _ _ _ _ _ _ has a major impact on many hospitality businesses. An example of this
    impact is _____

(continued)

12. Dangerous political c _ _ _ _ _ _ _ _ _ discourage t _ _ _ _ _. An example that shows the affect of this on the hospitality business is _____

13. A r _ _ _ _ _ _ _ _ or c _ _ _ _ _ _ _ _ _ _ is a period when the economy is slowing down and doing poorly. An e _ _ _ _ _ _ _ _ is a period when the economy is growing and doing well. During the 1990s, the hospitality industry in the United States did very well because

_____

14. The process in which the economies of different nations become interconnected is called g _ _ _ _ _ _ _ _ _ _ _ _ _. It is composed of _____

15. In the hospitality business, a t _ _ _ _ refers to the direction in which customer preferences are moving. How do hospitality managers use these? _____

_____

16. The study of characteristics of a population of people is called d _ _ _ _ _ _ _ _ _ _ _ _. A d _ _ _ _ _ _ _ _ _ _ _ t _ _ _ _ is the increase or decrease over time in the number of people in a subgroup. An example of this type of trend is _____

_____

17. A s _ _ _ _ _ _ t _ _ _ _ is a change in the structure or beliefs of a society. An example of this type of trend is _____

18. A l _ _ _ _ _ _ _ _ _ t _ _ _ _ _ is a change in the way people live their lives. The concern for h _ _ _ _ _ is one example. Another example is _____

_____

19. Trends in t _ _ _ _ _ _ _ _ _ _ affect many aspects of people's lives. The invention of the railroad, automobile, and airplane changed the hospitality industry. Name three other inventions that changed the hospitality industry. _____

_____

_____

20. A restaurant or hotel m _ _ _ _ _ _ wants to know about trends when planning a new restaurant or hotel. Name two restaurant trends and two hotel trends. _____

_____

_____

The World of Food and Beverages

Kick Off!

Activity A

Chapter 4

Name _____

Date _____ Period _____

Part 1

Read each statement below. Write *yes* or *no* in the *Agree?* column. Be ready to explain your reasons for each answer.

Statement	Agree?	Text Supports?
1. The food and beverage business and the foodservice business are two different types of businesses.		
2. There is only one way to categorize food and beverage businesses: commercial and institutional.		
3. Commercial foodservices compete for customers.		
4. Quick-service restaurants include fast-food restaurants, cafeterias, buffets, and carryout restaurants.		
5. In full-service restaurants, customers help themselves to food.		
6. Catering is the provision of food and service for a special event.		

(continued)

Statement	Agree?	Text Supports?
7. An example of institutional foodservice is your school cafeteria.		
8. People who use institutional foodservices usually have many other choices of where to dine.		
9. Sometimes, a consumer business will offer foodservice.		
10. The concept of a restaurant is what makes it different from another restaurant.		

Part 2

Look in the text to find support for each statement. If the text supports a statement, write *yes* in the *Text Supports?* column. Then write the text page number in the space below the statement. If the text does not support the statement, write *no* in the *Text Supports?* column. Then, in the space below the statement, rewrite the statement so that it is supported by the text.

Hospitality Terms Chapter 4

Name _____

Date _____ Period _____

Create a knowledge chart for each of the terms in Chapter 4. Each term is listed in Column A. For each term, write what you already know about the term in Column B. After you have studied Chapter 4, write what you have learned about the term in Column C.

A. Chapter 4 Terms	B. What I Already Know	C. What I Learned
1. food and beverage business		
2. foodservice		
3. commercial foodservice		
4. restaurant		
5. quick-service restaurant		
6. fast-food restaurant		
7. cafeteria		
8. buffet		
9. carryout restaurant		
10. full-service restaurant		
11. fine-dining restaurant		
12. casual dining restaurant		

(continued)

A. Chapter 4 Terms	B. What I Already Know	C. What I Learned
13. catering		
14. institutional foodservice		
15. institution		
16. in-house foodservice		
17. contract foodservice		
18. foodservice within a consumer business		
19. restaurant concept		
20. theme		
21. ambiance		
22. market		
23. market segment		
24. target market		

Categorizing Foodservice

Name _____

Date _____ Period _____

Part 1

Categorize the following foodservice operations as commercial or institutional foodservice by writing the correct letter in each blank. Use **C** for commercial foodservice examples and **I** for institutional foodservice examples.

_____ 1. Fast-food restaurant.

_____ 2. Hospital foodservice.

_____ 3. Foodservice on an army base.

_____ 4. Restaurant in a hotel.

_____ 5. Elegant downtown restaurant.

_____ 6. School foodservice.

Part 2

Commercial foodservices are often organized into the following four categories:

    catering

    full-service restaurant

    hotel and club foodservice

    quick-service restaurant

For each foodservice example listed below, write the category to which it belongs in the space provided.

_____ 7. Banquet at a private home.

_____ 8. Restaurant with seated service that serves Chinese food.

_____ 9. Snack bar in your health club.

_____ 10. Restaurant where you place your order, pay, and pick up your order at a counter.

_____ 11. Restaurant with a chef on staff, seated service, and a dress code.

_____ 12. Restaurant in which you walk along a service line, and the servers give you the dishes you request.

_____ 13. Dinner brought to your hotel room.

_____ 14. Business that provides prepared meals to pick up and eat somewhere else.

(continued)

Part 3

Provide complete answers to each of the following questions and statements.

15. List the three kinds of institutional foodservice and give one example of each.

_____

_____

_____

_____

_____

_____

_____

_____

_____

16. Name the three categories of foodservice within a consumer business and give one example of each.

_____

_____

_____

_____

_____

_____

_____

_____

_____

17. If you were to start your own foodservice business, what type would you choose? Explain your reasons.

_____

_____

_____

_____

_____

_____

_____

_____

Revisiting Chapter 4

Name _____

Date _____ Period _____

Choose from the words listed below to complete each sentence. Write the correct word in the blank in front of the sentence it completes.

buffet	commercial	customers	functions
cafeteria	concept	fast-food	institutional
casual dining	consumer business	feedback	market segment
catering	contract	foodservice	quick-service
comment	convenience	full-service	target market

_____ 1. A _____ business prepares, packages, serves, sells, or provides food for people to eat.

_____ 2. Food and beverage businesses that compete for customers are known as _____ foodservice.

_____ 3. A _____-_____ restaurant provides customers with convenience, speed, and basic service at low prices.

_____ 4. A _____-_____ restaurant has a counter where you place your order and wait to pick it up.

_____ 5. A _____ is a foodservice in which customers take trays to various stations along the serving line and request desired foods.

_____ 6. At a _____, customers walk along tables of displayed food and serve themselves.

_____ 7. A _____-_____ restaurant seats customers, takes their food orders, and serves the food to the customers at their tables.

_____ 8. Single-item restaurants, such as a pizza or pancake restaurant, are good examples of _____ _____ restaurants.

_____ 9. The provision of food and service for a special event is known as _____.

_____ 10. The three categories of _____ foodservice include schools, health care, and business.

_____ 11. When an institution hires an outside foodservice company to run its foodservice, this is known as _____ foodservice.

_____ 12. Business foodservice consists of foodservice provided in a business for the _____ of people who work at the business.

_____ 13. Recreation, retail, and transportation are the three categories of foodservice within a _____ _____.

(continued)

_____ 14. All food and beverage businesses must perform the same 12 _____.

_____ 15. A restaurant's _____ includes its theme, target market, location, decor, ambiance, and service style.

_____ 16. A market includes all the people who are potential _____.

_____ 17. Teenagers are a _____ _____ based on age.

_____ 18. A business strives to meet the needs of its _____ _____, or chosen market subgroup.

_____ 19. Guest _____ cards are a common way to obtain information about customer satisfaction.

_____ 20. Managers need customer _____ in order to increase customer satisfaction.

● Food Preparation and Service

Kick Off!

Activity A

Chapter 5

Name _____

Date _____ Period _____

Part 1

Read each statement below. Write *yes* or *no* in the *Agree?* column. Be ready to explain your reasons for each answer.

Statement	Agree?	Text Supports?
1. The menu is the basic game plan for a restaurant.		
2. The only factor to consider when planning a menu is taste.		
3. Institutional foodservices are more concerned about nutrition than commercial foodservices.		
4. Restaurants use standardized recipes to maintain consistency.		
5. It does not matter how the food is presented on the plate.		
6. The five basic styles of service are over-the-counter, drive-through, cafeteria, buffet, and seated.		

(continued)

Statement	Agree?	Text Supports?
7. American service, also called plate service, is a style of seated service.		
8. Food is served from the customer's left side with the server's left hand.		
9. Dirty dishes are removed from the customer's right side with the server's right hand.		
10. A busser's main job is to remove dirty dishes from the table.		

Part 2

Look in the text to find support for each statement. If the text supports a statement, write *yes* in the *Text Supports?* column. Then write the text page number in the space below the statement. If the text does not support the statement, write *no* in the *Text Supports?* column. Then, in the space below the statement, rewrite the statement so that it is supported by the text.

Hospitality Terms Chapter 5

Name _____

Date _____ Period _____

For each term in this chapter, develop a term overview. This term overview consists of the following three parts: a. your own definition, b. the textbook definition, and c. a sentence using the term. The first one is done for you.

1. menu

   a. Define the term in your own words.

   Your choices of food and drink at a restaurant

   b. Write the definition from the textbook.

   A list of food and beverages served in a restaurant.

   c. Write a sentence using the term.

   The chef planned the menu for the restaurant.

2. party

   a. Define the term in your own words.

   _____

   _____

   b. Write the definition from the textbook.

   _____

   _____

   c. Write a sentence using the term.

   _____

   _____

3. nutrients

   a. Define the term in your own words.

   _____

   _____

   b. Write the definition from the textbook.

   _____

   _____

   c. Write a sentence using the term.

   _____

   _____

(continued)

4. food production

   a. Define the term in your own words.

   _____

   _____

   b. Write the definition from the textbook.

   _____

   _____

   c. Write a sentence using the term.

   _____

   _____

5. consistency

   a. Define the term in your own words.

   _____

   _____

   b. Write the definition from the textbook.

   _____

   _____

   c. Write a sentence using the term.

   _____

   _____

6. recipe

   a. Define the term in your own words.

   _____

   _____

   b. Write the definition from the textbook.

   _____

   _____

   c. Write a sentence using the term.

   _____

   _____

7. yield

   a. Define the term in your own words.

   _____

   _____

(continued)

b. Write the definition from the textbook.

_____

_____

c. Write a sentence using the term.

_____

_____

8. standardized recipe

a. Define the term in your own words.

_____

_____

b. Write the definition from the textbook.

_____

_____

c. Write a sentence using the term.

_____

_____

9. food presentation

a. Define the term in your own words.

_____

_____

b. Write the definition from the textbook.

_____

_____

c. Write a sentence using the term.

_____

_____

10. plating

a. Define the term in your own words.

_____

_____

b. Write the definition from the textbook.

_____

_____

(continued)

c. Write a sentence using the term.

_____

_____

11. portion control

a. Define the term in your own words.

_____

_____

b. Write the definition from the textbook.

_____

_____

c. Write a sentence using the term.

_____

_____

12. garnish

a. Define the term in your own words.

_____

_____

b. Write the definition from the textbook.

_____

_____

c. Write a sentence using the term.

_____

_____

13. serving

a. Define the term in your own words.

_____

_____

b. Write the definition from the textbook.

_____

_____

c. Write a sentence using the term.

_____

_____

Menu Planning

Name _____

Date _____ Period _____

Food Selections		
apple pie	fruit cocktail	onion soup
applesauce	fruit strudel	pita bread
baklava	garlic bread sticks	pork chops
beef burritos	grapefruit half	potatoes, mashed
beef short ribs, barbecued	hot chocolate	quiche
broccoli	ice cream	rice
carbonated beverages	jambalaya	salmon, grilled
carrots	lamb kabobs	shrimp curry
cheese lasagna	lemon sorbet	steak, broiled
cheese soup	lemonade	string beans
chicken, fried	lentil soup	sweet potatoes
chocolate chip cookies	milk	tea
coffee	minestrone soup	tortillas
cornbread	mixed vegetables	tossed salad
cranberry gelatin salad	nachos	turkey, roasted
dinner rolls	okra	vegetable sticks with yogurt dip

The chart above provides a list of food selections. From these foods, develop a menu for one dinner meal. Make sure the menu is pleasing in taste and appearance. Write your food selections for each menu part in Column B in the chart below. In Column C, identify the food group for each food you choose. Some selections contain foods from more than one food group. Use Figure 5-8 of MyPyramid in the text to help you or visit **www.mypyramid.gov**. Then answer the questions on the next page.

A. Menu Part	B. Food Selection	C. Food Group(s)
Appetizer		
Soup		
Salad		
Entree		
Side Dishes		
Dessert		
Beverage		

(continued)

1. Why did you choose these particular foods for your dinner menu? Describe how your food choices go together in terms of taste and appearance.

_____

_____

_____

_____

2. Is your meal selection more appropriate for commercial or institutional foodservice? Why?

_____

_____

_____

_____

3. What type of pricing would you recommend for your menu? Why?

_____

_____

_____

_____

Revisiting Chapter 5

Activity D

Chapter 5

Name _____

Date _____ Period _____

Write complete answers to the following questions and statements in the space provided.

1. What tool is used as the basic game plan for a restaurant? _____
   _____

2. List the four types of menus based on how frequently the same foods are offered. _____
   _____
   _____

3. List the seven classic parts of a menu. _____
   _____
   _____

4. Name the method of pricing in which each food is priced and ordered separately. _____
   _____

5. Name the method of pricing in which a complete meal is offered at a set price. _____
   _____

6. List the six factors that must be considered when a restaurant plans a menu. _____
   _____
   _____
   _____

7. Why do people eat? Give two reasons. _____
   _____
   _____

8. Why are standardized recipes so important in restaurant food production? _____
   _____
   _____

9. List the five items a standardized recipe should include. _____
   _____
   _____
   _____

10. List two techniques of food preparation. _____
    _____
    _____

(continued)

11. List three cooking methods. _____
_____

12. List the three aspects of food presentation. _____
_____
_____

13. What makes plating food different from painting? _____
_____
_____

14. How can the cook make sure each portion is the same size? _____
_____
_____

15. What should the chef keep in mind when planning the artistic appearance of food on a plate?
_____
_____

16. In what way are over-the-counter, cafeteria, and buffet service similar? _____
_____
_____

17. List three popular types of seated service. _____
_____

18. List the four general categories of items in a place setting. _____
_____
_____

19. Why do the specific items in a place setting vary? _____
_____
_____

20. When you serve a table of people, which category of guest should be served first? _____
_____

21. Write the saying that will help you remember the direction for serving food. _____
_____
_____

22. Write the saying that will help you remember the direction for clearing dishes. _____
_____
_____

● Front- and Back-of-the-House

Kick Off!

<table>
<tr><td>**Activity A**</td><td>Name _____</td></tr>
<tr><td>**Chapter 6**</td><td>Date _____ Period _____</td></tr>
</table>

Part 1

Read each statement below. Do you agree with the statement? Write *yes* or *no* in the *Agree?* column. Be ready to explain your reasons for each answer.

Statement	Agree?	Text Supports?
1. In a restaurant, the front-of-the-house and the back-of-the-house rarely work together.		
2. The general manager is responsible for the entire restaurant.		
3. The front-of-the-house is responsible for the following six functions: seating, selling food, transmitting orders, serving customers, bussing tables, and obtaining payment from customers.		
4. Residence time is the time it takes for a family of four to travel from home to the restaurant, get seated, eat, and return home.		
5. A point-of-sales system (POS) complicates the transmission of orders to the kitchen.		

(continued)

Statement	Agree?	Text Supports?
6. The front-of-the-house staff consists of the restaurant manager, hosts or hostesses, servers, bussers, and cashiers.		
7. The back-of-the-house is responsible only for preparing food.		
8. The top manager in the kitchen of a unit of a chain restaurant is the executive chef.		
9. Without the steward and the dishwashing crew, a restaurant would come to a complete standstill.		
10. Food preparers include chefs, cooks, and expediters.		

Part 2

Look in the text to find support for each statement. If the text supports a statement, write *yes* in the *Text Supports?* column. Then write the text page number in the space below the statement. If the text does not support the statement, write *no* in the *Text Supports?* column. Then, in the space below the statement, rewrite the statement so that it is supported by the text.

Hospitality Terms Chapter 6

Name _____

Date _____ Period _____

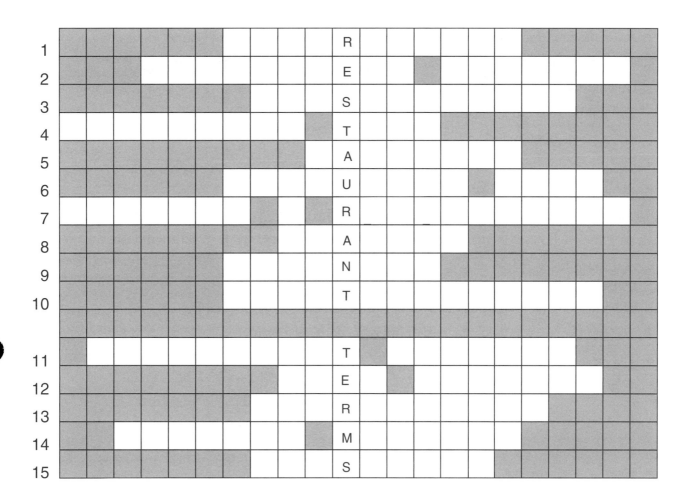

Complete the puzzle by writing the correct answers in the spaces. Use the definitions below for clues.

1. A promise to hold something, such as seating, for a customer.
2. When customers call a restaurant to have their names put onto a waiting list.
3. A window or area equipped with heat lamps to keep food hot until served.
4. The time it takes a family to eat a meal, pay a bill, and leave the restaurant.
5. Customers who arrive at a restaurant without a reservation.
6. The top manager in a restaurant or hotel kitchen.
7. The process of taking a reservation.
8. The process of finding seats for customers in a restaurant.
9. Related to cooking and kitchens.
10. Computerized system for recording an order at the place where the order is taken.
11. Employee who is responsible for everything that happens in the front-of-the-house.
12. Approach taken by casual dining restaurants that allows customers to walk in the door and expect to be seated.
13. The practice of taking more reservations than there are tables available.
14. The top manager in the kitchen of a unit of a chain restaurant.
15. The assistant to the executive chef.

(continued)

Part 2

For each term listed below, write a sentence using the term in the context of foodservice.

16. server

17. busser

18. dishwasher

19. steward

20. cook

21. chef

22. expediter

Restaurant Organization

Activity C

Chapter 6

Name _____

Date _____ Period _____

In a restaurant, jobs are available at many different levels. Your job is to fill in this organizational chart of restaurant employees using the job titles from the word bank below.

Assistant Manager

Bussers

Cashiers

Chefs or Cooks

Dishwashers

Executive Chef

General Manager

Host or Hostess

Restaurant Manager

Servers

Sous-Chef

Steward

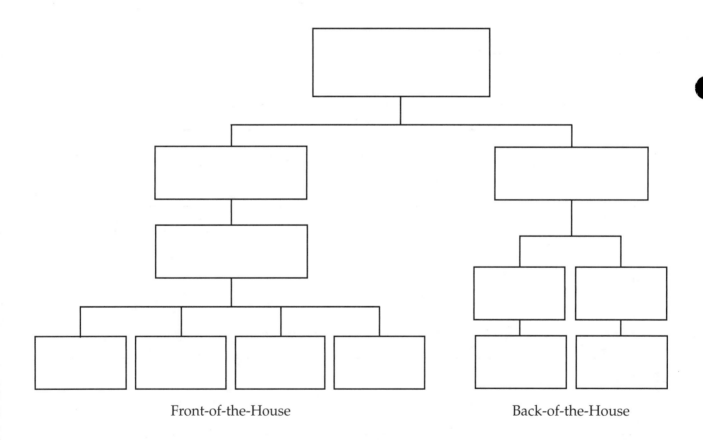

Front-of-the-House   Back-of-the-House

Revisiting Chapter 6

Name _____

Date _____ Period _____

Part 1

For each function listed below, determine whether it belongs to the front-of-the-house or the back-of-the-house. Write an **F** in the blank before each front-of-the-house function and a **B** in the blank before each back-of-the-house function.

_____ 1. accounting

_____ 2. bussing tables

_____ 3. engineering and maintenance

_____ 4. food production

_____ 5. human resources

_____ 6. marketing and sales

_____ 7. obtaining payment from customers

_____ 8. purchasing and receiving

_____ 9. seating guests

_____ 10. selling food

_____ 11. serving customers

_____ 12. transmitting orders to the kitchen

Part 2

Read the following story. In each blank, write the term from the word bank that correctly completes the corresponding blank in the sentence.

cooks	expediter	overbooking	reservation	server
culinary	general	pass-through	residence	sous-chef
dishwasher	host	point-of-sales	restaurant	steward

A. _____

Hope was recently hired as __(A)__ manager of the Paradise Restaurant. She is a little nervous because she will be in charge of the entire restaurant. Hope will supervise both the front- and back-of-the-house employees—even the other managers. One of her first tasks will be to familiarize herself with the restaurant's staff and operations.

(continued)

B. _____

C. _____

D. _____

E. _____

F. _____

G. _____

H. _____

I. _____

J. _____

K. _____

L. _____

M. _____

N. _____

O. _____

On her first day, Hope meets the restaurant's trainer, Salvador. Salvador tells Hope that seating at the Paradise is done primarily by __(B)__, or promising in advance to hold seating for a guest. With this type of seating, the restaurant predicts a __(C)__ time for each reserved table, or time it will likely take a party to eat the meal, pay the bill, and leave the restaurant. This practice helps the restaurant avoid __(D)__ reservations, or promising seating to more customers than is available at a given time.

Salvador introduces Hope to the __(E)__ manager, who is responsible for the front-of-the-house operations. Hope also meets the __(F)__, whose job it is to welcome customers and ensure they are promptly seated. Salvador shows Hope the Paradise's computerized table management system.

Next, Salvador reviews with Hope how orders are transmitted to the kitchen. He shows her the __(G)__-_____-_____ system, a wireless handheld unit with touch screens. These POS units are used by the __(H)__, whose job it is to record guests' food orders and transmit them to the kitchen. After the order is entered on the POS, it then goes to the kitchen, where it is printed.

Hope asks Salvador for a tour of the kitchen, where the __(I)__ staff works. On their way there, Salvador points out the __(J)__-_____, or area where food sits under a heat lamp until it is served. Hope asks how servers at the Paradise know when plates have been placed in this area for pickup. Salvador shows her how the POS alerts the server when an order is ready.

In the kitchen, Hope meets the executive chef and her assistant, the __(K)__-_____. She sees the __(L)__ is busy checking the stock of clean dishes and flatware. The __(M)__ is cleaning a large pan in the pot sink. Hope sees the chefs and __(N)__ preparing food at various stations in the kitchen. Finally, Hope meets the __(O)__, the person who gets the orders to the station chefs and checks all the orders before they are picked up by the servers.

With so many names and procedures to remember, Hope feels a little overwhelmed! She is still excited, however, about how much she will learn in this new role. Hope thanks Salvador for the tour. She knows that as she continues to learn her way around the Paradise, she will have many more questions for Salvador!

Hotel Food and Beverage Services

Kick Off!

Activity A	Name _____
Chapter 7	Date _____ Period _____

Part 1

Read each statement below. Write *yes* or *no* in the *Agree?* column. Be ready to explain your reasons for each answer.

Statement	Agree?	Text Supports?
1. Most hotels just offer coffee and sweet rolls in the lobby.		
2. Hotel dining rooms and kitchens have little in common with independent restaurants.		
3. There are two types of banquets: business banquets and social banquets.		
4. Banquets are usually booked through the sales department or the sales and catering department.		
5. The banquet staff consists only of the banquet manager and servers.		
6. The banquet chef is a critical part of the banquet team but is technically a part of the kitchen staff.		

(continued)

Statement	Agree?	Text Supports?
7. Four popular styles of banquet service are standing buffet, passed-items function, seated buffet, and seated banquet.		
8. Room service is the delivery of food and beverages to guests in their rooms.		
9. The beverage department is responsible for all the bars in the hotel.		
10. Bartenders and beverage servers are not responsible for the amount of alcohol that guests consume.		

Part 2

Look in the text to find support for each statement. If the text supports a statement, write *yes* in the *Text Supports?* column. Then write the text page number in the space below the statement. If the text does not support the statement, write *no* in the *Text Supports?* column. Then, in the space below the statement, rewrite the statement so that it is supported by the text.

Hospitality Terms Chapter 7

Activity B   Name _____

Chapter 7   Date _____ Period _____

Part 1

One way to learn about a term is to analyze it for words or word parts that you already know. You will develop a term analysis for each word below. The term analysis has four parts: a. list of the words or parts of words in the term that you recognize, b. list of other terms that contain one or more of the words or word parts, c. definition based on this analysis, and d. the definition from the textbook. The first one is done for you.

1. food and beverage director

    a. Write the words or word parts that you recognize.

    food, beverage, direct

    b. Write other terms that you know that contain these words or word parts.

    direction, directed, directly

    c. Write a definition based on your analysis of the words and word parts.

    someone who directs activities related to food and beverages

    d. Write the definition from the textbook.

    the manager in charge of all the food and beverage services in a hotel

2. station

    a. Write the words or word parts that you recognize.

    _____

    b. Write other terms that you know that contain these words or word parts.

    _____

    c. Write a definition based on your analysis of the words and word parts.

    _____

    _____

    d. Write the definition from the textbook.

    _____

    _____

3. passed-items function

    a. Write the words or word parts that you recognize.

    _____

    b. Write other terms that you know that contain these words or word parts.

    _____

(continued)

c. Write a definition based on your analysis of the words and word parts.

_____

_____

d. Write the definition from the textbook.

_____

_____

4. room service manager

a. Write the words or word parts that you recognize.

_____

b. Write other terms that you know that contain these words or word parts.

_____

c. Write a definition based on your analysis of the words and word parts.

_____

_____

d. Write the definition from the textbook.

_____

_____

5. hospitality suite

a. Write the words or word parts that you recognize.

_____

b. Write other terms that you know that contain these words or word parts.

_____

c. Write a definition based on your analysis of the words and word parts.

_____

_____

d. Write the definition from the textbook.

_____

_____

6. minibar

a. Write the words or word parts that you recognize.

_____

b. Write other terms that you know that contain these words or word parts.

_____

c. Write a definition based on your analysis of the words and word parts.

_____

_____

(continued)

d. Write the definition from the textbook.

_____

_____

7. bartender

a. Write the words or word parts that you recognize.

_____

b. Write other terms that you know that contain these words or word parts.

_____

c. Write a definition based on your analysis of the words and word parts.

_____

_____

d. Write the definition from the textbook.

_____

_____

Part 2

Each of the following pairs of terms have one word in common. However, each term has its own meaning. For each pair below, explain the difference between the two terms.

8. banquet _and_ banquet event order

_____

_____

9. banquet manager _and_ banquet chef

_____

_____

10. banquet servers _and_ banquet setup staff

_____

_____

11. seated buffet _and_ seated banquet

_____

_____

12. front bar _and_ service bar

_____

_____

(continued)

Part 3

Match each term below to its definition. Write the term in the blank in front of its definition.

_____ 13. A large meeting, usually sponsored by a group for its members.

_____ 14. Another term for _customers_; often used in reference to banquet customers.

_____ 15. A special event.

_____ 16. A table linen that is placed around buffet tables to hide the table legs.

_____ 17. In reference to a banquet, to clear dishes and food, clean tables and chairs, put away all furniture and equipment, and clean the floor.

_____ 18. The delivery of food and beverages to guests in their hotel rooms.

_____ 19. A place that serves alcoholic and nonalcoholic beverages.

_____ 20. A bar that is usually set up for one particular event, such as a banquet.

_____ 21. The person who usually oversees the hotel's front bars, service bars, special-purpose bars, room service beverage deliveries, hospitality suite bars, and minibars.

_____ 22. The person responsible for making sure the bar is stocked with liquor, ice, glassware, and supplies.

_____ 23. Person who takes orders for beverages, gives the orders to the bartender, then serves the drinks and takes payment.

bar

bar back

beverage manager

beverage server

break down

clients

convention

function

room service

skirting

special-purpose bar

Banquet Event Order

Name _____

Date _____ Period _____

Imagine you are the banquet manager for a local hotel. Choose one of the following events: prom, wedding, class reunion, birthday party, chess convention, graduation, or charity dance. Plan the event. Record the decisions in the banquet event order below.

Description of Event: Describe the event. Include the following: day, date, time of day, purpose, type of service, theme or ambiance.

_____

_____

_____

_____

_____

_____

_____

Kitchen Instructions: Describe the menu and any special food-related requests.

_____

_____

_____

_____

_____

_____

_____

Decor and Table Settings: Describe how the room will be decorated. Include a sample of place setting in the box on the next page. Include information about centerpieces and any other room decorations.

_____

_____

_____

_____

_____

_____

_____

(continued)

Place Setting

Setup Instructions: Describe how the room should be set up. Include a room diagram in the box below.

Room Setup

Audiovisual Instructions: Describe the audiovisual equipment needed and any special lighting requests. Arrangements for a band or DJ go here.

Revisiting Chapter 7

Name _____

Date _____ Period _____

The following departments are involved in hotel foodservice:

Banquet

Beverage

Room service

Sales

Below is a list of tasks that are done as part of hotel foodservice. In the blank before each task, write the name of the department responsible for that task.

_____ 1. Check minibars daily.

_____ 2. Provide special effects.

_____ 3. Provide menus for guest rooms.

_____ 4. Work with the client to arrange the details of a banquet.

_____ 5. Set up special-purpose bars.

_____ 6. Write the banquet event order and schedule banquet workers.

_____ 7. Prepare timelines for banquets.

_____ 8. Feed large groups in the hotel.

_____ 9. Sell the meeting facilities.

_____ 10. Monitor alcohol consumption of guests.

_____ 11. Serve food and beverages during a banquet.

_____ 12. Set up audiovisual equipment.

_____ 13. Check halls for dirty trays and dishes.

_____ 14. Hire and train beverage staff.

_____ 15. Set up standing buffets.

_____ 16. Clear dirty dishes.

_____ 17. Pick up menus during the night.

_____ 18. Take orders for beverages.

_____ 19. Create the ambiance of the event.

_____ 20. Skirt the tables.

_____ 21. Set tables.

_____ 22. Prepare beverages.

_____ 23. Serve at passed-items functions.

(continued)

_____ 24. Set up appropriate tables, chairs, and service equipment.

_____ 25. Make sure each banquet runs smoothly.

_____ 26. Check identification of guests who appear younger than 30.

_____ 27. Ensure that equipment is safe.

_____ 28. Check on temperature comfort of guests.

_____ 29. Break down the banquet room.

_____ 30. Clean tables and chairs before storing.

_____ 31. Enforce local and state liquor laws.

_____ 32. Clean floors.

_____ 33. Deliver food to guests' rooms.

_____ 34. Follow a diagram for room set up.

_____ 35. Supervise room service operations.

_____ 36. Stock the bar with ice, glassware, and supplies.

_____ 37. Obtain fresh flowers for a wedding reception.

_____ 38. Set up a hospitality suite.

_____ 39. Hire part-time staff when several banquets occur in the same week.

_____ 40. Book banquets.

● Purchasing and Receiving

Kick Off!

Activity A   Name _____

Chapter 8   Date _____ Period _____

Part 1

Read each statement below. Write *yes* or *no* in the *Agree?* column. Be ready to explain your reasons for each answer.

Statement	Agree?	Text Supports?
1. A purchaser makes sure that a business has everything it needs in the right amounts at the right time.		
2. When you hear a person ask for the "specs" for an item, they are asking for the special wrapping for the product.		
3. Most food products are available in a variety of quality levels.		
4. Cost-effective buying consists of buying large quantities of perishables.		
5. Suppliers are constantly developing new products to meet restaurant needs.		
6. When supplies are received, they are immediately put into storage.		

(continued)

Statement	Agree?	Text Supports?
7. Improperly stored foods and other items can spoil and become unusable.		
8. FIFO—first in, first out—is a key concept in using stored foods.		
9. Storerooms should be open at specific times and locked at all other times.		
10. The process of keeping track of items in inventory is called inventory control.		

Part 2

Look in the text to find support for each statement. If the text supports a statement, write *yes* in the *Text Supports?* column. Then write the text page number in the space below the statement. If the text does not support the statement, write *no* in the *Text Supports?* column. Then, in the space below the statement, rewrite the statement so that it is supported by the text.

Hospitality Terms Chapter 8

Activity B   Name _____

Chapter 8   Date _____ Period _____

For each term in this chapter, develop a term overview. This term overview consists of the following three parts: a. your own definition, b. the textbook definition, and c. a situation in the hospitality industry in which the term would be used. The first one is done for you.

1. purchasing

   a. Define the term in your own words.

   Buying something.

   b. Write the definition from the textbook.

   Buying of goods and services for use in a business.

   c. Describe a situation in the hospitality industry in which this term would be used.

   A sales representative visits a hotel chain headquarters. He asks for the purchasing department.

2. receiving

   a. Define the term in your own words.

   _____

   _____

   b. Write the definition from the textbook.

   _____

   _____

   c. Describe a situation in the hospitality industry in which this term would be used.

   _____

   _____

3. storage

   a. Define the term in your own words.

   _____

   _____

   b. Write the definition from the textbook.

   _____

   _____

   c. Describe a situation in the hospitality industry in which this term would be used.

   _____

   _____

(continued)

4. inventory

    a. Define the term in your own words.

_____

_____

    b. Write the definition from the textbook.

_____

_____

    c. Describe a situation in the hospitality industry in which this term would be used.

_____

_____

5. purchaser

    a. Define the term in your own words.

    b. Write the definition from the textbook.

_____

_____

    c. Describe a situation in the hospitality industry in which this term would be used.

_____

_____

6. specification

    a. Define the term in your own words.

_____

_____

    b. Write the definition from the textbook.

_____

_____

    c. Describe a situation in the hospitality industry in which this term would be used.

_____

_____

7. in stock

    a. Define the term in your own words.

_____

_____

    b. Write the definition from the textbook.

_____

_____

(continued)

c. Describe a situation in the hospitality industry in which this term would be used.

_____

_____

8. perishable

a. Define the term in your own words.

_____

_____

b. Write the definition from the textbook.

_____

_____

c. Describe a situation in the hospitality industry in which this term would be used.

_____

_____

9. supplier

a. Define the term in your own words.

_____

_____

b. Write the definition from the textbook.

_____

_____

c. Describe a situation in the hospitality industry in which this term would be used.

_____

_____

10. purchase order

a. Define the term in your own words.

_____

_____

b. Write the definition from the textbook.

_____

_____

c. Describe a situation in the hospitality industry in which this term would be used.

_____

_____

(continued)

11. shipment

    a. Define the term in your own words.

_____

_____

    b. Write the definition from the textbook.

_____

_____

    c. Describe a situation in the hospitality industry in which this term would be used.

_____

_____

12. invoice

    a. Define the term in your own words.

_____

_____

    b. Write the definition from the textbook.

_____

_____

    c. Describe a situation in the hospitality industry in which this term would be used.

_____

_____

13. FIFO

    a. Define the term in your own words.

_____

_____

    b. Write the definition from the textbook.

_____

_____

    c. Describe a situation in the hospitality industry in which this term would be used.

_____

_____

Purchasing and Receiving Line-Up

Activity C

Chapter 8

Name _____

Date _____ Period _____

Foodservice businesses follow many steps when purchasing and receiving food products. These steps are listed below, but they need to be reorganized into the correct order. Write a **1** in the blank of the lettered item that happens first, a **2** in the blank of the lettered item that happens second, and so on.

_____ A. store nonperishable foods

_____ B. note unacceptable items from shipment

_____ C. store perishable foods

_____ D. check shipment against invoice

_____ E. select supplier

_____ F. receive invoice

_____ G. write specifications

_____ H. get bids

_____ I. unload shipment at receiving dock

_____ J. issue requested items

_____ K. receive credit memorandum

_____ L. request items from storage by completing requisition form

_____ M. write purchase order

_____ N. store supplies

Which step of the purchasing and receiving process do you think you would least enjoy doing, and why?

_____

_____

_____

_____

Which step of the purchasing and receiving process do you think you would most enjoy doing, and why?

_____

_____

_____

_____

Revisiting Chapter 8

Activity D

Chapter 8

Name _____

Date _____ Period _____

(continued)

Across

5. A _____ inventory is a written count of each item that is updated whenever items are issued or received.

6. A _____ is a list of products that a business wants to purchase.

10. *Credit slip* is another name for a _____ _____.

11. A delivery _____ is a piece of paper prepared by a supplier that lists the quantities and types of items delivered.

12. When an item is _____ _____, it is on hand in the kitchen or storeroom.

14. A set of items delivered from one supplier at one time is called a _____.

16. Abbreviation for storage technique that uses older items first and newer items last.

18. Another name for requisitioning is _____.

22. The _____ _____ is the place where deliveries are received.

23. A _____ order is a form used to submit a request for goods from a supplier.

24. A requisition _____ is used to request items from inventory.

25. A reorder _____ is the minimum amount of an item in storage; the quantity at which the item must be reordered.

27. A detailed description of a product that is needed is called a _____.

Down

1. A _____ is an expert in buying goods and services for a business.

2. The process of placing items in a safe, secure place until they are needed is called _____.

3. The process of making items available to employees is _____.

4. Any product that spoils quickly is called _____.

5. A _____ _____ is the process of taking count in which a person goes to the storage areas and counts each item by hand.

7. The process of making sure the items that were delivered are those that were ordered is called _____.

8. In _____-_____ buying, the purchaser seeks to buy the most products at the best quality needed for the least amount of money.

9. The buying of goods and services for use by a business is called _____.

13. A _____ is a business from which supplies are purchased.

15. The maximum amount of an item that is allowed to be held in storage at any one time is called the _____ _____.

17. _____ foods are those that have been opened and stored in other containers.

19. The process of counting and recording all the items in storage is called _____.

20. A bill prepared by the supplier is called an _____.

21. Inventory _____ is the process of keeping track of items in inventory.

26. A _____ is a document that states what a particular supplier will charge for a specific product.

Food Safety and Sanitation

Kick Off!

Activity A   Name _____

Chapter 9   Date _____ Period _____

Part 1

Read each statement below. Write *yes* or *no* in the *Agree?* column. Be ready to explain your reasons for each answer.

Statement	Agree?	Text Supports?
1. An occurrence of a foodborne illness can ruin a foodservice business.		
2. The three types of food contaminants are physical, chemical, and biological.		
3. In most situations, a small number of bacteria is not harmful.		
4. The temperature danger zone is the range of temperatures that is harmful to bacteria.		
5. This is no difference between cleaning and sanitizing.		
6. The most important way to prevent foodborne illness is by proper hand washing.		

(continued)

Statement	Agree?	Text Supports?
7. Gloves provide no protection if they become contaminated, for example, if a person touches a contaminated surface while wearing gloves.		
8. The two basic rules of food handling are (1) Keep cold foods cold. (2) Keep hot foods hot.		
9. Federal, state, and local governments are unconcerned about food safety.		
10. The general manager of a restaurant and the food and beverage manager in a hotel are responsible for the safety and sanitation of their operations.		

Part 2

Look in the text to find support for each statement. If the text supports a statement, write *yes* in the *Text Supports?* column. Then write the text page number in the space below the statement. If the text does not support the statement, write *no* in the *Text Supports?* column. Then, in the space below the statement, rewrite the statement so that it is supported by the text.

Hospitality Terms Chapter 9

Activity B

Name _____

Chapter 9

Date _____ Period _____

For each term in this chapter, develop a term overview. This term overview consists of the following three parts: a. your own definition, b. the textbook definition, and c. a sentence using the term. The first one is done for you.

1. contaminant

   a. Define the term in your own words.

   Something that doesn't belong.

   b. Write the definition from the textbook.

   A substance in food that does not belong there.

   c. Write a sentence using the term.

   Food should not have any contaminants in it.

2. foodborne illness

   a. Define the term in your own words.

   b. Write the definition from the textbook.

   c. Write a sentence using the term.

3. contaminated food

   a. Define the term in your own words.

   b. Write the definition from the textbook.

   c. Write a sentence using the term.

(continued)

Copyright Goodheart-Willcox Co., Inc.

Chapter 9 Food Safety and Sanitation **81**

4. pathogen

   a. Define the term in your own words.

_____

_____

   b. Write the definition from the textbook.

_____

_____

   c. Write a sentence using the term.

_____

_____

5. potentially hazardous food

   a. Define the term in your own words.

_____

_____

   b. Write the definition from the textbook.

_____

_____

   c. Write a sentence using the term.

_____

_____

6. temperature danger zone

   a. Define the term in your own words.

_____

_____

   b. Write the definition from the textbook.

_____

_____

   c. Write a sentence using the term.

_____

_____

7. transmit

   a. Define the term in your own words.

_____

_____

(continued)

   b. Write the definition from the textbook.

_____

_____

   c. Write a sentence using the term.

_____

_____

8. personal hygiene

   a. Define the term in your own words.

_____

_____

   b. Write the definition from the textbook.

_____

_____

   c. Write a sentence using the term.

_____

_____

9. cleaning

   a. Define the term in your own words.

_____

_____

   b. Write the definition from the textbook.

_____

_____

   c. Write a sentence using the term.

_____

_____

10. sanitizing

   a. Define the term in your own words.

_____

_____

   b. Write the definition from the textbook.

_____

_____

(continued)

_____

c. Write a sentence using the term.

_____

_____

11. food contact surface

   a. Define the term in your own words.

   _____

   _____

   b. Write the definition from the textbook.

   _____

   _____

   c. Write a sentence using the term.

   _____

   _____

12. cross-contamination

   a. Define the term in your own words.

   _____

   _____

   b. Write the definition from the textbook.

   _____

   _____

   c. Write a sentence using the term.

   _____

   _____

13. Hazard Analysis Critical Control Point (HACCP)

   a. Define the term in your own words.

   _____

   _____

   b. Write the definition from the textbook.

   _____

   _____

   c. Write a sentence using the term.

   _____

   _____

Keeping Foods Safe

Activity C   Name _____

Chapter 9   Date _____ Period _____

Read the following statements about food handling practices in the foodservice industry. If the statement is true, write a *T* in the blank before the statement. If the statement is false, make the statement true by rewriting the underlined words in the space below the statement.

_____ 1. A major cause of foodborne illnesses is careless employees <u>who wash their hands constantly with antibacterial soap.</u>

_____

_____

_____ 2. An incident of foodborne illness can <u>ruin a restaurant.</u>

_____

_____ 3. Examples of <u>physical contaminants</u> include pesticides, cleaning agents, and metals.

_____

_____ 4. Biological contaminants are <u>microscopic living substances</u> that accidentally get into food.

_____

_____ 5. Restaurant managers are more concerned about <u>viruses</u> than any other pathogens.

_____

_____ 6. The temperature danger zone is the range between <u>10°F and 150°F.</u>

_____

_____ 7. A parasite is an organism that must live in another <u>living thing</u> in order to survive.

_____

_____ 8. Personal hygiene consists of the actions a person takes <u>to perform his or her job properly.</u>

_____

_____

_____ 9. When working with food, it is important to keep nails <u>short and maintained.</u>

_____

_____ 10. Hands should be washed every time you touch <u>food.</u>

_____

_____ 11. <u>Sweat</u> is a source of food contamination.

_____

(continued)

_____ 12. Silverware should be stored in drawers so the server can pick it up by the <u>handle</u>.

_____ 13. Ice should be picked up with <u>your hands</u> and scooped into the glasses.

_____ 14. Reliable food suppliers <u>combine</u> food products and general supplies during shipping.

_____ 15. When food products are received, the package should be dated and placed <u>in front of</u> the other items in storage.

_____ 16. The major ways to control pests are through <u>good housekeeping and pesticides</u>.

_____ 17. Dishwashing is a two-part job in a foodservice kitchen: <u>first sanitize, then clean</u>.

_____ 18. <u>Thermostats</u> are used to check the temperature of foods during cooking.

_____ 19. Cross-contamination occurs when <u>a raw food is placed on a surface, and then a cooked food is placed on the same surface.</u>

_____ 20. Safe holding of cold foods requires keeping them at a temperature of <u>55°F or below</u>.

_____ 21. Safe holding of hot foods requires keeping them at a temperature of <u>160°F or above after cooking.</u>

_____ 22. Restaurants are periodically inspected by local health departments to make sure they meet <u>food safety and sanitation</u> requirements.

_____ 23. HACCP provides a system for assuring <u>the appeal of food.</u>

_____ 24. A critical control point is a point at which <u>nothing</u> can be done to prevent a food hazard.

_____ 25. <u>The general manager of a restaurant and the food and beverage manager in a hotel are</u> responsible for the safety and sanitation of their operations.

Preventing Hazards

Name _____

Date _____ Period _____

Read the following case study. Underline the words that describe a situation that is potentially hazardous. Then complete the table below. In Column A, list each potentially hazardous situation. In Column B, explain why each situation is hazardous. In Column C, describe what should be done to prevent the hazard. There are seven situations.

Main High School's debating team decided to meet at a local restaurant to celebrate their victory. Rosaria, team captain, noticed the host was wearing a dirty apron. The dirt on the apron looked like blood from raw meat. Rosaria asked the host about it. The host laughed and said he had been working in the kitchen because a cook hadn't shown up. Rosaria then asked if the team could sit together. The host said, "Of course." He then wiped his hands on the apron and started placing silverware on the tables.

Rosaria and Jacob were talking as they waited, when suddenly they heard a crash. A server had just spilled a tray of food on the table where they were going to sit. The server started cleaning up the mess. She sneezed and grabbed the cloth hanging from her apron to cover her mouth. She then used the cloth to wipe the table.

Rosaria was a little concerned, so she looked toward the kitchen. Through the kitchen door, she could see the refrigerator door was open, but no one was near it. A large container of potato salad was sitting on a counter. A cook was standing over a grill, with hair hanging down around her face. The cook wiped her brow with her hand and continued cooking. Rosaria looked back at the team and said, "Hey, everyone. My mom said we could go to my house. Want to go?"

Potentially Hazardous Situations and Solutions		
A. Potentially Hazardous Situation	B. Why?	C. What Should Be Done to Avoid Hazard
1.		
2.		
3.		
4.		
5.		
6.		
7.		

Revisiting Chapter 9

Read each statement below. Fill in the letters for the missing words. Then either complete the statement or answer the question.

1. Food that is c _ _ _ _ _ _ _ _ _ _ _ _ can cause illnesses. The three types of

   c _ _ _ _ _ _ _ _ _ _ _ _ are _____

   _____

2. A p _ _ _ _ _ _ _ contaminant is any item that accidentally gets into food. Three exam-

   ples are _____

   _____

3. A c _ _ _ _ _ _ _ contaminant consists of c _ _ _ _ _ _ _ _ _ that are toxic or not

   usually found in food. Three examples are _____

   _____

   _____

4. A b _ _ _ _ _ _ _ _ _ contaminant is a microscopic living substance that accidentally

   gets into food. Three examples are _____

   _____

5. The five main symptoms of foodborne illness caused by p _ _ _ _ _ _ _ _ _ are

   _____

   _____

   _____

6. The type of contaminants responsible for most foodborne illnesses are the

   b _ _ _ _ _ _ _ _ _ contaminants. Which is the most common cause of foodborne

   illness? _____

7. B _ _ _ _ _ _ _ reproduce rapidly under ideal conditions. In what temperature range

   do they reproduce the fastest? _____

8. The t _ _ _ _ _ _ _ _ _ _ _ d _ _ _ _ _ z _ _ _ is the range of temperatures

   between _ _ °F and _ _ _ °F. Why is this range of temperatures given this name?

   _____

   _____

(continued)

9. A virus is a microorganism that can be t _ _ _ _ _ _ _ _ _ _ _ from one person to another on food. How does food help a virus make a person sick? _____

_____

_____

10. A p _ _ _ _ _ _ _ is an organism that must live in another living thing in order to survive. List three animals that humans eat as food that these organisms also live in.

_____

_____

11. There are three main ways that f _ _ _ _ _ _ _ _ illnesses can be prevented. List them.

_____

_____

_____

12. The actions that a person takes to keep his or her body and clothing clean and to remove pathogens are known as p _ _ _ _ _ _ _ _ h _ _ _ _ _ _ _. List three of these actions.

_____

_____

_____

13. Foods must be handled properly during s _ _ _ _ _ _ _ and s _ _ _ _ _ _. What can happen to foods during theses processes? _____

_____

14. Contamination cannot be detected by the senses. However, food that is s _ _ _ _ _ _ _ can be detected by the senses. Describe how the senses detect food that is s _ _ _ _ _ _ _.

_____

_____

15. P _ _ _ _ _ such as rodents and insects can cause serious problems for a restaurant. The two major ways to control them are through _____

_____

16. The physical removal of soil and food residues from surfaces of equipment, utensils, tables, and floors is known as c _ _ _ _ _ _ _ _. Sanitizing is _____

_____

(continued)

17. The purpose of <u>d</u> _ _ _ _ _ _ _ _ _ _ _ is to clean and sanitize equipment, utensils,

    and <u>d</u> _ _ _ _ _ _ _ _. Why is this one of the most important jobs in the foodservice

    industry? _____

    _____

18. Food handling most often refers to procedures that prevent the growth of

    <u>b</u> _ _ _ _ _ _ _ _ in foods. What are the two basic rules of food handling? _____

    _____

    _____

19. To keep foods out of the <u>t</u> _ _ _ _ _ _ _ _ _ _ _ <u>d</u> _ _ _ _ _ _ <u>z</u> _ _ _ _, the

    <u>t</u> _ _ _ _ _ _ _ _ _ _ _ of the food must be measured. What tool is used for this meas-

    uring? _____

20. <u>C</u> _ _ _ _ _ _-<u>c</u> _ _ _ _ _ _ _ _ _ _ _ _ _ _ occurs when microorganisms in one food

    are transferred to another food. State the two main rules for preventing this. _____

    _____

    _____

21. <u>C</u> _ _ _ _ _ _ _ _, <u>t</u> _ _ _ _ _ _ _ _, and <u>r</u> _ _ _ _ _ _ _ _ _ are processes during

    which foods go through the temperature danger zone. What can be done to prevent food-

    borne illnesses from foods that go through these processes?

    _____

    _____

22. Four <u>f</u> _ _ _ _ _ _ _ <u>a</u> _ _ _ _ _ _ _ _ have a major responsibility for food safety:

    FSIS, FDA, APHIS, and EPA. Write the complete name of each agency. _____

    _____

    _____

    _____

23. A local <u>h</u> _ _ _ _ _ <u>d</u> _ _ _ _ _ _ _ _ _ _ _ <u>i</u> _ _ _ _ _ _ _ _ _ will inspect a

    restaurant for food safety and sanitation <u>v</u> _ _ _ _ _ _ _ _ _ _ _. What might happen to

    the restaurant if violations are found?_____

    _____

(continued)

24. HACCP stands for <u>H</u> __ __ __ __ __   <u>A</u> __ __ __ __ __ __ __ __   <u>C</u> __ __ __ __ __ __ __

    <u>C</u> __ __ __ __ __ __ __   <u>P</u> __ __ __ __. What is HACCP? _____

    _____

25. The g __ __ __ __ __ __ __ manager of a restaurant and the <u>f</u> __ __ __ and <u>b</u> __ __ __ __ __ __ __ __

    manager in a hotel are responsible for the <u>s</u> __ __ __ __ __ and <u>s</u> __ __ __ __ __ __ __ __ __ __ of

    their operations. List three things these managers do to carry out their responsibilities. _____

    _____

    _____

    _____

Chapter 9   Food Safety and Sanitation   **91**

The World of Lodging

Kick Off!

Activity A

Chapter 10

Name _____

Date _____ Period _____

Part 1

Read each statement below. Do you agree with the statement? Write *yes* or *no* in the *Agree?* column.
Be ready to explain your reasons for each answer.

Statement	Agree?	Text Supports?
1. The only way to organize the lodging industry is based on level of service.		
2. There are four categories of lodging businesses based on level of service: full-service hotels, limited-service properties, specialty accommodations, and institutional housing.		
3. Full-service hotels are small and offer few services.		
4. Senior housing provides places for seniors in college to live.		
5. Lodging properties are often categorized based on location.		
6. Like restaurants, lodging properties have three types of ownership: independent, chain, and franchise.		

(continued)

Statement	Agree?	Text Supports?
7. An affiliation group is a group of independent hotels that creates a central office for reservations and marketing.		
8. The lodging market can be divided into six major segments: business, conventions and meetings, leisure, budget, long-stay, and special.		
9. Lodging properties usually do not provide foodservice.		
10. The concept of a lodging property makes it different from other lodging properties.		

Part 2

Look in the text to find support for each statement. If the text supports a statement, write *yes* in the *Text Supports?* column. Then write the text page number in the space below the statement. If the text does not support the statement, write *no* in the *Text Supports?* column. Then, in the space below the statement, rewrite the statement so that it is supported by the text.

Hospitality Terms Chapter 10

Name _____

Date _____ Period _____

For each definition given below, write in the term it describes. The letters *H, O, T, E,* and *L* have been filled in for you where they occur.

1. A hotel that provides the highest level of amenities, service, room furnishings, public spaces, and technology.
   l _ _ _ _ _   h o t e l

2. The whole idea of the lodging property or chain.
   l o _ _ _ _ _ _   _ _ o _ _ e _ t

3. The price actually charged to a guest for one night's lodging.
   _ o o _   _ _ t e

4. Hotels that have the lowest rates and least service.
   _ _ _ _ _ e t   h o t e l _

5. A variety of accommodations that are not hotels, motels, or institutional housing.
   _ _ e _ _ _ l t _   _ _ _ _ o _ _ o _ _ t _ o _ _

6. A large sleeping room filled with beds for many guests.
   _ o _ _ _ t o _ _

7. A large hotel that provides a complete range of services.
   _ _ l l - _ e _ _ _ _ e   h o t e l

8. A hotel that is smaller, provides fewer services, and is less expensive than a full-service hotel.
   l _ _ _ t e _ - _ e _ _ _ _ e   _ _ o _ e _ t _

9. A group of independent hotels that creates a central office for reservations and marketing.
   _ _ _ _ _ l _ _ t _ o _   _ _ o _ _

10. A hotel that caters to the vacationer or leisure traveler.
    _ e _ o _ t   h o t e l

11. A lodging facility where 60 percent or more of the total occupancy is generated by conferences.
    _ o _ _ e _ e _ _ e   _ e _ te _

12. The percentage of each market segment that is staying at a lodging property.
    _ _ e _ t   _ _ _ _

13. An exhibit during which people show and sell their goods and services.
    t _ _ _ e   _ h o _

14. Another name for an affiliation group or consortium.
    _ e _ e _ _ _ l   _ _ _ _ t e _

15. Housing that is provided for people who live in institutions.
    _ _ _ _ t _ t _ t _ o _ _ l   h o _ _ _ _ _ _

16. A meal that consists of breakfast foods that do not need to be cooked.
    _ o _ t _ _ e _ t _ l   _ _ e _ _ _ _ _ t

(continued)

17. A place that provides entertainment, recreation, and relaxation for vacationers.
 __ e __ o __ t

18. A private home offering one or more guest rooms.
 __ e __ - __ __ __ - __ __ e __ __ __ __ __ t

19. Places for people over 55 to live.
 __ e __ __ o __   h o __ __ __ __ __

20. A hotel that is designed to provide for the special needs of conventions and trade shows.
 __ o __ __ e __ t __ o __   h o t e l

21. Hotels that offer a medium level of service and a midrange price.
 l __ __ __ t e __ - __ e __ __ __ __ e h o t e l __

22. Another name for an *affiliation group* or *referral group*.
 __ o __ __ o __ t __ __ __

23. An inexpensive place to stay where sleeping rooms, bathrooms, and kitchen facilities are shared.
 h o __ t e l

24. The day-to-day running of a hotel.
 h o t e l __ __ __ __ __ __ e __ e __ t

25. The space where a trade show is held.
 e __ __ __ __ __ __ t h __ l l

26. A room rate that includes meals.
 __ e __ l __ l __ __

27. A hotel staff member who helps guests make arrangements and advises guests on what to do and see in the area around the hotel.
 __ o __ __ __ e __ __ e

28. A hotel accommodation that consists of more than one room.
 __ __ __ t e

29. A large building designed specifically to hold large meetings, conventions, and trade shows.
 __ o __ __ e __ t __ o __ __ e __ t e __

30. The official rate for one night's lodging at a lodging property.
 __ __ __ __ __ __ t e

The Winning Team in the World of Lodging

Activity C   Name _____

Chapter 10   Date _____ Period _____

Read the case study and answer the questions below in the space provided.

The Grove Town High School debate team has won a district championship and is preparing to go to state competition. The competition will be held at a university in a city four hours away. As the coach, it's your job to find lodging for the team. Dormitory rooms on the campus are not available. The team will travel in the school van and can stay some distance from the university, if needed. Your budget is limited, but adequate if four people share each room. You will need a total of eight rooms to house all the team members and adult chaperones. You will need to stay at least one night, but possibly as many as three nights. The length of your stay will depend on whether any of the team members qualify for final rounds.

1. What types of lodging do you anticipate will be available and within your budget? Check all that apply.

_____ bed-and-breakfast operations   _____ conference centers   _____ limited-service hotels

_____ budget hotels   _____ convention hotels   _____ lodges

_____ campgrounds   _____ extended-stay hotels   _____ luxury hotels

_____ condominium hotels   _____ full-service hotels   _____ motels

                                             _____ hostels   _____ resort hotels

2. Place an **N** in the blank for any of the following services your team will need during their stay. Place a **W** by other services team members might desire if cost allows.

_____ banquet facilities   _____ Internet access   _____ room service

_____ casual restaurant   _____ kitchen facilities   _____ spa services

_____ concierge   _____ luggage assistance   _____ TV and telephone in room

_____ continental breakfast   _____ meal plan   _____ valet parking

_____ daily housekeeping   _____ parking close to room   _____ vending machines

_____ elegant building and rooms   _____ recreational facilities (tennis, pool, golf, work-out room)

_____ fine-dining restaurant

_____ handicap accommodations   _____ refrigerator and microwave

(continued)

3. Which of the following levels of service and price ranges do you think will best meet your team's needs: luxury, first-class, midrange, economy, or budget? Explain.

_____

_____

_____

_____

_____

4. Based on the information above, which type of lodging do you think is most likely to meet your team's needs? Explain.

_____

_____

_____

_____

_____

Revisiting Chapter 10

Activity D

Chapter 10

Name _____

Date _____ Period _____

Provide complete answers to each of the following questions and statements.

1. List the four categories of lodging businesses based on level of service.

   _____

   _____

2. What two features distinguish a full-service hotel from other hotels?

   _____

   _____

3. List the five subcategories of full-service hotels.

   _____

   _____

   _____

4. Describe three key features of a limited-service property.

   _____

   _____

   _____

5. Explain the difference between a limited-service hotel and a budget hotel.

   _____

   _____

   _____

6. List five groups of specialty accommodations.

   _____

   _____

   _____

7. Describe two types of senior housing.

   _____

   _____

8. List five main locations for a lodging business.

   _____

   _____

   _____

(continued)

9. Describe three types of hotel ownership.

_____

_____

10. What is the purpose of an affiliation group?

_____

_____

11. What does a hotel management company do?

_____

12. Give the size ranges for small, medium, and large lodging properties.

_____

_____

13. Describe how the level of service provided by a lodging property influences the price charged.

_____

_____

14. How might location of a lodging property affect the price?

_____

_____

15. Explain the difference between a rack rate and a room rate.

_____

16. Name three situations in which a hotel might offer special rates.

_____

_____

17. List the six major market segments in the lodging industry.

_____

_____

18. Explain the difference between target market and guest mix.

_____

_____

19. What is a meal plan?

_____

_____

_____

20. What is the purpose of a lodging concept?

_____

_____

CHAPTER 11

● Front Office

Kick Off!

Activity A

Chapter 11

Name _____

Date _____ Period _____

Part 1

Read each statement below. Do you agree with the statement? Write *yes* or *no* in the *Agree?* column. Be ready to explain your reasons for each answer.

Statement	Agree?	Text Supports?
1. The rooms division is the part of the hotel that handles all tasks involved in preparing and selling convention rooms.		
2. The rooms division is often divided into four departments: front office, housekeeping, security, and engineering.		
3. A property management system (PMS) is a manual system used to run lodging properties.		
4. The front office handles everything related to selling sleeping rooms and interacting with guests.		
5. The front office is often divided into four departments: reservations, uniformed services, telecommunications, and front desk.		

(continued)

Statement	Agree?	Text Supports?
6. The uniformed services staff helps the security officers handle disturbances.		
7. The telecommunications department handles telephone service in the hotel.		
8. The front desk is command central for a lodging property.		
9. The main responsibilities of the front desk agent are guest check-in and guest checkout.		
10. The front office manager has no special tasks of particular importance.		

Part 2

Look in the text to find support for each statement. If the text supports a statement, write *yes* in the *Text Supports?* column. Then write the text page number in the space below the statement. If the text does not support the statement, write *no* in the *Text Supports?* column. Then, in the space below the statement, rewrite the statement so that it is supported by the text.

Hospitality Terms Chapter 11

Activity B

Chapter 11

Name _____

Date _____ Period _____

Part 1

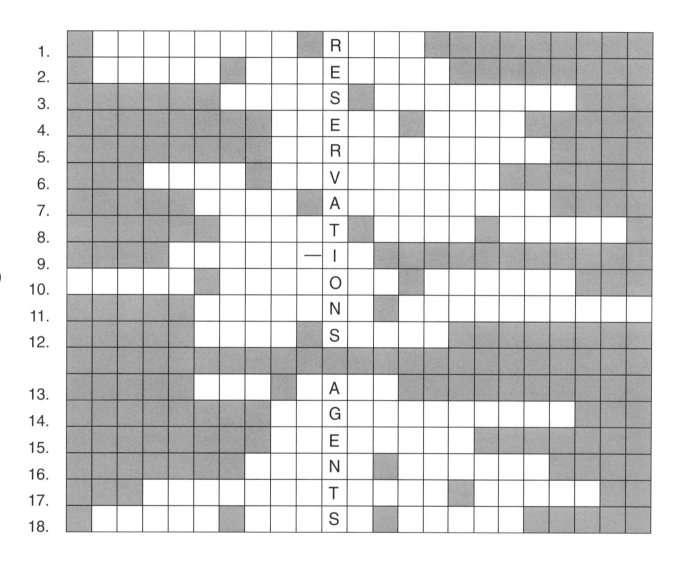

(continued)

_____

Use the clues below to fill in the missing words in the puzzle.

1. Room where guests sleep for one or more nights.
2. Manager in charge of the rooms division.
3. The part of the hotel that handles all tasks involved in preparing and selling sleeping rooms.
4. Another name for *sleeping room*.
5. Predicting the number of guests who will stay at the hotel.
6. Count of the number of rooms sold and number of rooms available each day.
7. Takes care of guests' needs as they arrive at the hotel.
8. Person who works at the front desk.
9. Process of registering guests, assigning rooms, and distributing keys.
10. Record kept by a lodging property that records information about each guest each time he or she stays at the property.
11. Process of correcting any errors on the bill, then taking payment from the guest.
12. Regular period of time in which work is done, such as 7 a.m. to 3 p.m.
13. Key used with an electronic system.
14. Process of keeping a list of everyone who is staying at the hotel.
15. Process of paying for rooms and returning keys.
16. The department in a hotel that interacts with guests and sells sleeping rooms.
17. Person who takes the call when guests call to reserve a room.
18. Stages of a hotel guest's relations with the hotel staff.

(continued)

Part 2

Read the story below. Then choose the words from the term bank to fill in the blanks in the story. Terms can be used more than once. Every term in the bank is used at least once.

bell attendant

central reservations center

check in

front desk

front desk agent

front office manager

function room

guaranteed reservation

guest folio

nonguaranteed reservation

property management system

registration record

reservation record

wake-up call

19. _____

20. _____

21. _____

22. _____

23. _____

24. _____

25. _____

26. _____

27. _____

28. _____

29. _____

30. _____

31. _____

32. _____

33. _____

34. _____

35. _____

36. _____

37. _____

The __(19)__ walked up to the confused-looking guest. "Would you like help with your bags?" she asked. The guest replied, "Yes. I need to __(20)__." They walked up to the __(21)__. The guest said to the __(22)__, "I have a reservation for tonight." The __(23)__ looked for the reservation in the __(24)__. The agent said, "There is no __(25)__ for you in the computer." The guest said, "That's impossible. I made a __(26)__ last week with my credit card. I called the hotel's __(27)__ in Phoenix." The agent said, "I'm sorry. Let me get the manager in charge, the __(28)__."

The __(29)__ asked, "What is the problem?" The guest answered, "I specifically made a __(30)__, not a __(31)__, because I wanted to be sure I had a place to sleep tonight." The __(32)__ answered, "I am very sorry. We have no rooms tonight. We have a big wedding in our __(33)__, and all our sleeping rooms are occupied. I will find a room for you in a nearby hotel."

When the guest arrived at the new hotel, he was quickly checked in. The front desk agent created a __(34)__ in the __(35)__ to show the guest was registered in the hotel. The agent also created a __(36)__ to keep a record of all the guest's charges and payments. Before the guest left to go to his room, the agent asked, "Would you like a __(37)__ tomorrow morning?" The guest replied, "Yes. At 7 a.m. I have an early business meeting to attend."

Functions of the Rooms Division

Name _____

Chapter 11

Date _____ Period _____

The rooms division is often divided into four departments:

Front office

Housekeeping

Security

Engineering

Consult Figure 11-2 in the text. For each task listed below, write the name of the department responsible for that task.

_____   1. Carpet cleaning.

_____   2. Wake-up calls.

_____   3. Taking reservations over the phone.

_____   4. Maintain swimming pools, hot tubs, and exercise equipment.

_____   5. Sell rooms.

_____   6. Clean the lobby of the hotel.

_____   7. Find a crib for a guest room.

_____   8. Recommend places to go sightseeing.

_____   9. Respond to a report of someone trying to open all the guest room doors.

_____ 10. Handle reservations sent by fax.

_____ 11. Take luggage from the car into the hotel.

_____ 12. Provide transportation to the airport.

_____ 13. Clean and sanitize public restrooms.

_____ 14. Transfer calls to guest rooms.

_____ 15. Wash laundry.

_____ 16. Fix a broken washing machine.

_____ 17. Provide extra towels to guests.

_____ 18. Break up a fight.

_____ 19. Maintain landscaping and golf courses.

_____ 20. Check-in and checkout.

_____ 21. Handle emergencies.

(continued)

_____ 22. Maintain elevators.

_____ 23. Clean and sanitize guest rooms.

_____ 24. Keep records of incidents and emergencies.

_____ 25. Fix a leaking faucet.

_____ 26. Clean hallways.

_____ 27. Repair a broken window.

_____ 28. Find a no-smoking room for a guest.

_____ 29. Take care of linens.

_____ 30. Washing windows.

The Hotel Guest Cycle

Name _____

Date _____ Period _____

The stages in the hotel guest cycle are listed below.

Prearrival

Arrival

Occupancy

Departure

Listed below are activities that occur during the hotel guest cycle. In the blank before each activity, write the name of the stage in which that activity occurs.

_____ 1. Sending a fax from the hotel business office.

_____ 2. Getting directions to the hotel.

_____ 3. Asking for wake-up calls.

_____ 4. Packing up the hotel room.

_____ 5. Playing tennis at the hotel's tennis court.

_____ 6. Buying beverages in the lounge.

_____ 7. Settling the account.

_____ 8. Parking the car.

_____ 9. Making a reservation.

_____ 10. Registering.

_____ 11. Selecting a lodging property.

_____ 12. Having breakfast delivered to the room.

_____ 13. Reviewing the bill.

_____ 14. Renting movies.

_____ 15. Taking luggage out of the car.

_____ 16. Eating at hotel restaurants.

_____ 17. Arranging transportation to the airport.

_____ 18. Paying the bill.

_____ 19. Asking the concierge for restaurant recommendations.

_____ 20. Shopping at the hotel shops.

_____ 21. Calling home from the telephone in the room.

_____ 22. Putting luggage back in the car.

_____ 23. Getting a haircut in hotel salon.

_____ 24. Using a Web site to learn about different hotels.

_____ 25. Requesting more towels from housekeeping.

Revisiting Chapter 11

Activity E

Chapter 11

Name _____

Date _____ Period _____

Respond to the statements or questions by writing an answer in the space below each one.

1. What is the main business of a lodging property? _____
   _____

2. Which division of the hotel is mainly responsible for this main business? _____
   _____

3. What is the difference between a guest room and a function room? _____
   _____
   _____
   _____

4. Name the three main functions of the rooms division. _____
   _____
   _____
   _____

5. Name the four departments into which the rooms division is often divided. _____
   _____
   _____
   _____
   _____

6. Name the computer system that a lodging property uses to keep track of information. _____
   _____

7. What are the two main functions of the front office? _____
   _____
   _____

8. Who manages the front office? _____

9. Why is the front office sometimes divided into four departments? _____
   _____
   _____
   _____

(continued)

10. List the four departments into which the front office can be divided. _____

_____

_____

_____

_____

11. List two main functions of the reservations department. _____

_____

_____

12. Name the staff members who will handle reservations if the property is too small to have a sep-
    arate reservations department. _____

_____

13. List the four major responsibilities of the uniformed services department. _____

_____

_____

_____

_____

14. What is the major responsibility of the telecommunications department? _____

_____

15. Why is the front desk so important to the lodging property? _____

_____

_____

16. List the two major responsibilities of the front desk agent. _____

_____

_____

17. If a property is small, for what other tasks will front desk agents be responsible? _____

_____

_____

18. List six categories of tasks that front desk agents do. _____

_____

_____

_____

_____

(continued)

19. Why is registration important? _____

_____

20. List the two main financial tasks for which the front desk is responsible. _____

_____

21. What responsibilities do front desk agents have for security? _____

_____

_____

22. What kinds of guest services do front desk agents provide? _____

_____

_____

23. List five personal qualities and skills that front office staff should have._____

_____

_____

24. List two tasks that are of particular importance for the front office manager. _____

_____

25. List the four stages in the hotel guest cycle. _____

_____

_____

_____

Housekeeping

Kick Off!

Activity A   Name _____

Chapter 12   Date _____ Period _____

Part 1

Read each statement below. Do you agree with the statement? Write *yes* or *no* in the *Agree?* column. Be ready to explain your reasons for each answer.

Statement	Agree?	Text Supports?
1. The housekeeping department has the smallest staff in the hotel.		
2. The three major functions of the housekeeping department are to keep the hotel clean, sanitary, and attractive.		
3. There is no difference between clean and sanitary.		
4. The room attendant's only responsibility is to collect dirty bed linens.		
5. The tasks of the room attendant can be divided into six groups: entering guest rooms, cleaning guest rooms, providing guest supplies, reporting problems, limiting guest room access, and turndown service.		

(continued)

Statement	Agree?	Text Supports?
6. After the room attendants finish cleaning the guest rooms, they go on to clean the public areas of the hotel.		
7. The three major tasks of the laundry department are washing laundry, care of linens, and inventory of linens.		
8. There are two types of housekeeping services: in-house and contract.		
9. The executive housekeeper has responsibility for training, scheduling staff, supplies and equipment, room status, and contact with the front desk.		
10. Throughout the day, the front office departments and the housekeeping department regularly communicate with each other.		

Part 2

Look in the text to find support for each statement. If the text supports a statement, write *yes* in the *Text Supports?* column. Then write the text page number in the space below the statement. If the text does not support the statement, write *no* in the *Text Supports?* column. Then, in the space below the statement, rewrite the statement so that it is supported by the text.

Hospitality Terms Chapter 12

Activity B　　　　　　　　　　　　　Name _____

Chapter 12　　　　　　　　　　　　　Date _____ Period _____

For each term in this chapter, develop a term overview. The term overview consists of three parts:
a. your own definition, b. the textbook definition, and c. a sentence using the term. The first one is
done for you.

1. housekeeping department

    a. Define the term in your own words.

    The department that cleans the guest rooms.

    b. Write the definition from the textbook.

    Responsible for keeping the hotel clean.

    c. Write a sentence using the term in the context of hotel housekeeping.

    The housekeeping department orders new cleaning supplies.

2. mildew

    a. Define the term in your own words.

    _____

    _____

    b. Write the definition from the textbook.

    _____

    _____

    c. Write a sentence using the term in the context of hotel housekeeping.

    _____

    _____

3. linens

    a. Define the term in your own words.

    _____

    _____

    b. Write the definition from the textbook.

    _____

    _____

    c. Write a sentence using the term in the context of hotel housekeeping.

    _____

    _____

(continued)

4. laundry

   a. Define the term in your own words.

_____

_____

   b. Write the definition from the textbook.

_____

_____

   c. Write a sentence using the term in the context of hotel housekeeping.

_____

_____

5. room attendant

   a. Define the term in your own words.

_____

_____

   b. Write the definition from the textbook.

_____

_____

   c. Write a sentence using the term in the context of hotel housekeeping.

_____

_____

6. executive housekeeper

   a. Define the term in your own words.

_____

_____

   b. Write the definition from the textbook.

_____

_____

   c. Write a sentence using the term in the context of hotel housekeeping.

_____

_____

7. cleaning cart

   a. Define the term in your own words.

_____

_____

(continued)

b. Write the definition from the textbook.

_____

_____

c. Write a sentence using the term in the context of hotel housekeeping.

_____

_____

8. consumables

   a. Define the term in your own words.

   _____

   _____

   b. Write the definition from the textbook.

   _____

   _____

   c. Write a sentence using the term in the context of hotel housekeeping.

   _____

   _____

9. public areas

   a. Define the term in your own words.

   _____

   _____

   b. Write the definition from the textbook.

   _____

   _____

   c. Write a sentence using the term in the context of hotel housekeeping.

   _____

   _____

10. linen room

    a. Define the term in your own words.

    _____

    _____

    b. Write the definition from the textbook.

    _____

    _____

(continued)

c. Write a sentence using the term in the context of hotel housekeeping.

_____

_____

11. scheduling

a. Define the term in your own words.

_____

_____

b. Write the definition from the textbook.

_____

_____

c. Write a sentence using the term in the context of hotel housekeeping.

_____

_____

12. occupied

a. Define the term in your own words.

_____

_____

b. Write the definition from the textbook.

_____

_____

c. Write a sentence using the term in the context of hotel housekeeping.

_____

_____

13. vacant

a. Define the term in your own words.

_____

_____

b. Write the definition from the textbook.

_____

_____

c. Write a sentence using the term in the context of hotel housekeeping.

_____

_____

Housekeeping

Name _____

Date _____ Period _____

Part 1

In the drawing of a sleeping room below, identify each space or item that should be cleaned and each item that should be sanitized. Write a **C** on items that need to be cleaned. Write a **C** and an **S** on items that need to be both cleaned and sanitized.

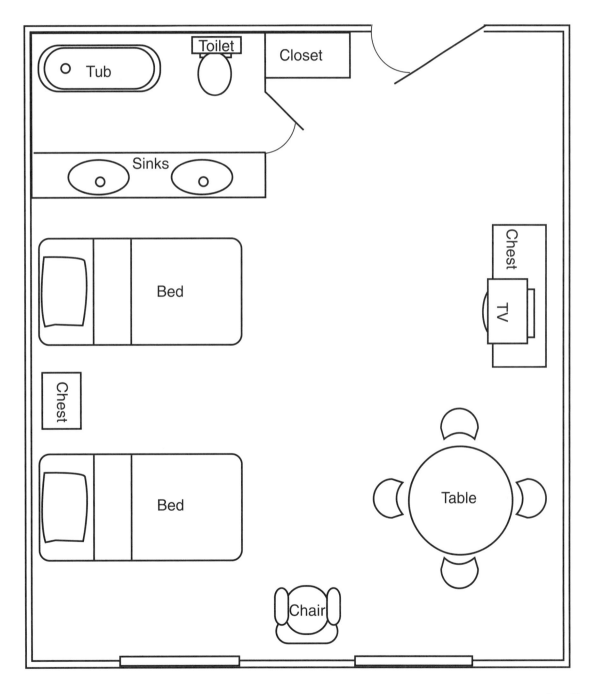

(continued)

Name

_____

Part 2

Read each piece of advice below as if you are preparing to train room attendants. Which would be good advice for you to give? Write **GA** in the blank for each piece of good advice. For each piece of bad advice, write **BA** in the blank and rewrite the advice to be good advice.

_____ 1. Before entering a room, always knock and say, "Housekeeping."

_____

_____ 2. If there is no answer after the first knock, enter the room.

_____

_____ 3. If there are guests in a room you enter, go ahead and clean the room anyway.

_____

_____ 4. Place the cleaning cart across the doorway to block others from entering.

_____

_____ 5. Turn on the lights, open the drapes, and set the air conditioner as soon as you enter the room.

_____

_____ 6. Gather items that stayover guests have left, and place these on the cart to be turned in.

_____

_____ 7. Clean ashtrays, mirrors, and furniture.

_____

_____ 8. Empty the vacuum cleaner bag into the room trash can.

_____

_____ 9. Place the bedspreads, pillows, and blankets on the floor while you make the bed.

_____

_____ 10. Remove dirty towels from the room and take to the laundry area immediately.

_____

_____ 11. Clean and sanitize the bathroom floor, tub, sink, and toilet.

_____

_____ 12. Restock supplies and towels as needed.

_____

_____ 13. Inspect the room and record anything that needs repairs.

_____

_____ 14. Leave drapes open, set air conditioner, and leave the room.

_____

_____ 15. Turn off the lights before leaving the room.

_____

Personal Application

Name _____

Date _____ Period _____

In each of the spaces below, write a description of jobs you have done in your home that would help you get a housekeeping job at a hotel. Consider what you have done in each of the following categories: cleanliness and sanitation; providing for guests; caring for public areas (for example, family room of your home); laundry; and contracting with other people to do jobs (for example, doing lawn work for pay).

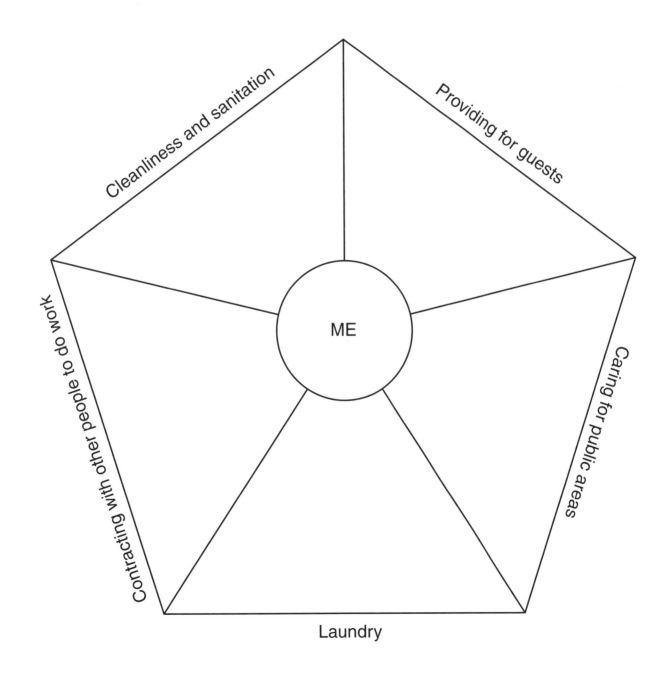

Revisiting Chapter 12

Activity E

Chapter 12

Name _____

Date _____ Period _____

Provide complete answers to each of the following questions and statements.

1. List the three major functions of the housekeeping department. _____
_____

2. Explain the difference between clean and sanitary. _____
_____
_____

3. Describe the process of sanitizing. _____
_____
_____

4. What is the name used for guest room items made of cloth? _____

5. Give two meanings for the word *laundry*. _____
_____

6. What is the job title for the person who cleans the guest rooms? _____
_____

7. What is the job title for the person who is the top manager in the housekeeping department?
_____

8. What is the job title for the team member who checks the guest room after it has been cleaned?
_____

9. What is the job title for the person who manages the room attendants and inspectors? _____
_____

10. List six tasks of the room attendant. _____
_____
_____

11. List eight consumables and explain why they have to be replaced regularly. _____
_____
_____
_____

12. What is the name of the service provided by first-class hotels in which the bed covers are prepared for the guests to sleep in and a chocolate is left on the pillow? _____

(continued)

13. List five public areas of hotels._____

_____

_____

14. List two titles used for workers who are responsible for cleaning the public areas of hotels.

_____

_____

15. What is the job title for the person who supervises the laundry attendants and the seamsters?

_____

16. For which tasks are seamsters responsible? _____

_____

17. For which tasks are laundry attendants responsible?_____

_____

_____

18. What are the three major tasks of the laundry department?_____

_____

_____

19. Which two employees are often responsible for the linen inventory?_____

_____

20. List four reasons linens might need to be replaced._____

_____

_____

_____

21. List the two types of housekeeping services used by hotels._____

_____

22. What term is used to describe a room with a guest registered to it?_____

23. What term is used to describe a room without a guest registered to it? _____

24. List two reasons guest rooms might have an out-of-order status. _____

_____

_____

25. The front office and housekeeping departments need to be in regular communication. List four topics they need to discuss. _____

_____

_____

Security

Kick Off!

Name _____

Date _____ Period _____

Part 1

Read each statement below. Do you agree with the statement? Write *yes* or *no* in the *Agree?* column. Be ready to explain your reasons for each answer.

Statement	Agree?	Text Supports?
1. Security consists of actions taken to prevent crime and to protect the safety of people and property.		
2. Security officers are the only ones responsible for security at a hospitality business.		
3. Security activities can be divided into four groups: structural security, security policies, surveillance, and safety and emergency procedures.		
4. Many security features can be built into a lodging property.		
5. Security policies include rules concerning employee ID cards, key control, limiting entrances, lost and found, and special procedures.		

(continued)

Statement	Agree?	Text Supports?
6. Security officers perform surveillance while on patrol.		
7. The security department has no responsibility during emergencies.		
8. Front desk agents often use two-way radios for faster communication with security staff.		
9. Employees outside the security department have no responsibilities for safety or security.		
10. Four of the tasks the director of security must perform are develop and implement safety and security policies, train employees, prepare staff schedules, and maintain equipment.		

Part 2

Look in the text to find support for each statement. If the text supports a statement, write *yes* in the *Text Supports?* column. Then write the text page number in the space below the statement. If the text does not support the statement, write *no* in the *Text Supports?* column. Then, in the space below the statement, rewrite the statement so that it is supported by the text.

Hospitality Terms Chapter 13

Activity B   Name _____

Chapter 13   Date _____ Period _____

For each term in this chapter, develop a term overview. The term overview consists of three parts: a. your own definition, b. the textbook definition, and c. a sentence using the term. The first one is done for you.

1. security

   a. Define the term in your own words.

   Being safe.

   b. Write the definition from the textbook.

   Actions taken to prevent crime and protect the safety of people and property.

   c. Write a sentence using the term.

   Hotels need a good security department.

2. liability

   a. Define the term in your own words.

   _____

   _____

   b. Write the definition from the textbook.

   _____

   _____

   c. Write a sentence using the term.

   _____

   _____

3. safe deposit box

   a. Define the term in your own words.

   _____

   _____

   b. Write the definition from the textbook.

   _____

   _____

   c. Write a sentence using the term.

   _____

   _____

(continued)

4. insurance

 a. Define the term in your own words.

 _____

 _____

 b. Write the definition from the textbook.

 _____

 _____

 c. Write a sentence using the term.

 _____

 _____

5. plainclothes security officer

 a. Define the term in your own words.

 _____

 _____

 b. Write the definition from the textbook.

 _____

 _____

 c. Write a sentence using the term.

 _____

 _____

6. uniformed security officer

 a. Define the term in your own words.

 _____

 _____

 b. Write the definition from the textbook.

 _____

 _____

 c. Write a sentence using the term.

 _____

 _____

7. structural security

 a. Define the term in your own words.

 _____

 _____

(continued)

b. Write the definition from the textbook.

_____

_____

c. Write a sentence using the term.

_____

_____

8. security policies

   a. Define the term in your own words.

   _____

   _____

   b. Write the definition from the textbook.

   _____

   _____

   c. Write a sentence using the term.

   _____

   _____

9. key control

   a. Define the term in your own words.

   _____

   _____

   b. Write the definition from the textbook.

   _____

   _____

   c. Write a sentence using the term.

   _____

   _____

10. surveillance

   a. Define the term in your own words.

   _____

   _____

   b. Write the definition from the textbook.

   _____

   _____

(continued)

c. Write a sentence using the term.

_____

_____

11. patrol

   a. Define the term in your own words.

_____

_____

   b. Write the definition from the textbook.

_____

_____

   c. Write a sentence using the term.

_____

_____

12. security log

   a. Define the term in your own words.

_____

_____

   b. Write the definition from the textbook.

_____

_____

   c. Write a sentence using the term.

_____

_____

13. accident report

   a. Define the term in your own words.

_____

_____

   b. Write the definition from the textbook.

_____

_____

   c. Write a sentence using the term.

_____

_____

Hospitality and Insurance

Activity C   Name _____

Chapter 13   Date _____ Period _____

Write complete answers to the following questions in the space provided.

1. Describe the purpose of insurance for a hospitality site. _____

   _____

   _____

   _____

2. List three kinds of insurance that hospitality businesses need. _____

   _____

   _____

   _____

3. Describe how insurance policies work. _____

   _____

   _____

   _____

4. Give an example of a situation for which property insurance would be beneficial. _____

   _____

   _____

   _____

5. List three examples of businesses being sued for liability. _____

   _____

   _____

   _____

6. What is the purpose of crime insurance? _____

   _____

   _____

   _____

7. Why are some locations charged more for insurance than others? _____

   _____

   _____

   _____

Revisiting Chapter 13

Activity D   Name _____

Chapter 13   Date _____ Period _____

Write complete answers to the following questions and statements in the space provided.

1. List five reasons security is critical in hospitality businesses. _____

    _____

    _____

    _____

    _____

2. Give three definitions for the term *security*. _____

    _____

    _____

3. What is the emphasis of security? _____

    _____

4. What is the major responsibility of security? _____

    _____

5. List three categories of threats to security. _____

    _____

    _____

6. Where should a guest place valuables to make the hotel responsible for losses if something is
    stolen? _____

    _____

7. What is the financial arrangement used to protect individuals or businesses from financial loss?

    _____

8. List the three types of insurance that most hospitality businesses buy. _____

    _____

    _____

9. What is the most important personal quality of a security officer? _____

10. List the four groups of security activities and give the purpose of each. _____

    _____

    _____

    _____

    _____

(continued)

11. What is the difference between structural security and the other types of security activities?

_____

_____

12. Give three examples of structural security. _____

_____

_____

13. List four examples of technology used in security. _____

_____

_____

14. List four security policies and explain how they improve security. _____

_____

_____

_____

_____

15. What are the three basic surveillance tasks of security officers? _____

_____

_____

_____

16. What responsibility does the security department have for emergencies? _____

_____

_____

17. What is the purpose of a security log? _____

_____

18. Name two departments that must work together to maintain guest security. _____

_____

_____

19. What responsibilities do hospitality employees outside the security department have for safety and security? _____

_____

_____

20. List the four security-specific tasks the director of security must carry out. _____

_____

_____

• Engineering

Kick Off!

Activity A	**Name** _____
Chapter 14	**Date** _____ **Period** _____

Part 1

Read each statement below. Do you agree with the statement? Write *yes* or *no* in the *Agree?* column. Be ready to explain your reasons for each answer.

Statement	Agree?	Text Supports?
1. The purpose of engineering is to keep the facility in top condition for safety, guest satisfaction, and profitability.		
2. Engineering has six functions: preventive maintenance, deep cleaning, repairs, remodeling, resource management, and emergencies.		
3. Preventive maintenance consists of the cleaning and repair of equipment that is in working order.		
4. Most hospitality businesses handle every repair as though it were an emergency.		
5. Remodeling is sometimes done to meet new laws, such as the Americans with Disabilities Act.		

(continued)

Statement	Agree?	Text Supports?
6. The engineering department is responsible for conservation.		
7. Engineering works with security during emergencies.		
8. The three main systems in a building are electrical, plumbing, and heating and air conditioning.		
9. Engineering is not responsible for recreational areas such as swimming pools, golf courses, and fitness rooms.		
10. The engineering department of a large hotel will include a chief engineer, skilled technicians, maintenance staff, and groundskeeping staff.		

Part 2

Look in the text to find support for each statement. If the text supports a statement, write *yes* in the *Text Supports?* column. Then write the text page number in the space below the statement. If the text does not support the statement, write *no* in the *Text Supports?* column. Then, in the space below the statement, rewrite the statement so that it is supported by the text.

Hospitality Terms Chapter 14

Activity B

Name _____

Chapter 14

Date _____ Period _____

Part 1

Match each term below to its definition. Write the term in the blank in front of its definition.

_____ 1. Thorough cleaning that involves extra time or equipment.

_____ 2. Heating, ventilation, and air conditioning systems.

_____ 3. The main chemical used to keep swimming pool water safe.

_____ 4. The top manager of the engineering department.

_____ 5. The person responsible for the upkeep of the grounds around a building.

_____ 6. The outside area around the building.

_____ 7. Another name for the chief engineer.

chief engineer

chlorine

deep cleaning

facility manager

grounds

groundskeeper

HVAC systems

remodeling

Part 2

Match each term below to its definition. Write the term in the blank in front of its definition.

_____ 8. The cleaning and repair of equipment that is in working order.

_____ 9. Safe drinking water.

_____ 10. Water that is not clean enough to drink but is still usable.

_____ 11. A measurement that indicates the level of acidity or alkalinity of water.

_____ 12. Another name for the chief engineer.

_____ 13. Work such as landscaping, watering, weed control, mowing, fertilizing, and trash removal.

_____ 14. The process of making the building and the grounds around it look appealing through the use of plants.

alkaline

groundskeeping

landscaping

nonpotable water

pH value

plant manager

potable water

preventive maintenance

Write About Engineering

Name _____

Date _____ Period _____

Imagine that you are a reporter for a local newspaper. Use the following outline to compose an article explaining the role of the chief engineer in a new hotel that has opened in your town.

Paragraph 1 (Introduction)

Lead sentence: The purpose of engineering in the hospitality business is _____

_____

_____

Thesis statement: The chief engineer is in charge of this department. His (or her) roles include _____

_____

_____

_____

Paragraphs 2-4 (Body)

Use topic sentences and supporting sentences for each paragraph about the three roles of the chief engineer.

_____

_____

_____

_____

_____

_____

_____

_____

_____

_____

_____

(continued)

Paragraph 5 (Conclusion)

Engineering is important to the hospitality business because _____

_____

_____

_____

_____

Revisiting Chapter 14

Activity D   Name _____

Chapter 14   Date _____ Period _____

Read the following statements about engineering in hospitality. If the statement is true, write *T* in the blank. If the statement is false, rewrite the underlined portion of the statement to make it true.

_____ 1. Much of the equipment in restaurants and hotels has the <u>potential to be hazardous</u>.

_____

_____ 2. The engineering department is responsible for some of the <u>least</u> expensive equipment on the property.

_____

_____ 3. In a hotel or restaurant, preventive maintenance is <u>only done when equipment starts to show need for repair</u>.

_____

_____

_____ 4. The <u>front office staff and the engineering department</u> often work together on deep-cleaning tasks.

_____

_____ 5. In order to install modern equipment such as Internet connections, businesses often have to do <u>repairs</u>.

_____

_____ 6. The <u>engineering department</u> is responsible for implementing methods of conservation.

_____

_____ 7. The engineering department works closely with <u>the security staff, front office staff, and municipal emergency services</u> during emergencies.

_____

_____

_____ 8. The <u>engineering department</u> must make sure that safety devices are in place and operating properly.

_____

_____ 9. <u>Nonpotable</u> water is commonly used for cooking, laundry, and drinking.

_____

(continued)

_____ 10. Roofs must be inspected regularly and repaired <u>if a hole occurs, shingles break, or other damage occurs</u>.

_____

_____

_____ 11. The two reasons for maintaining the parking lot are <u>to make a good first impression and prevent injuries</u>.

_____

_____

_____ 12. Hotel room attendants and house staff must be on the alert for <u>maintenance problems</u>.

_____

_____ 13. Swimming pools should be closed <u>once every six months</u> for thorough cleaning, repainting, and repair.

_____

_____ 14. Chlorine levels of a pool at a hotel should be checked <u>once per week</u>.

_____

_____ 15. Fitness rooms need to be properly cleaned and sanitized to protect guests from <u>chemicals</u>.

_____

_____ 16. Large hotels may have a <u>groundskeeping department</u> that is separate from engineering, while smaller hotels will have it as part of engineering.

_____

_____ 17. Golf courses require <u>maintenance</u> that is different from the lawn care of the hotel.

_____

_____ 18. Restaurants normally require <u>more</u> engineering services than hotels do.

_____

_____ 19. The role of the chief engineer is to <u>train, supervise, and motivate</u> employees in the engineering department.

_____

_____ 20. Restaurants and small lodging properties use <u>outside services</u> for many engineering tasks.

_____

● Business Basics

Kick Off!

Activity A	Name _____	
Chapter 15	Date _____ Period _____	

Part 1

Read each statement below. Do you agree with the statement? Write *yes* or *no* in the *Agree?* column. Be ready to explain your reasons for each answer.

Statement	Agree?	Text Supports?
1. Business structure refers only to the number of units in the business.		
2. There are only three forms of business ownership.		
3. A corporation is a form of business ownership.		
4. The only kind of work done in a hospitality business is the work itself.		
5. A franchise is a unit of a chain with a different owner.		
6. Management has five major functions: planning, organizing, staffing, leading, and controlling.		

(continued)

Statement	Agree?	Text Supports?
7. Leadership is the ability to boss people around.		
8. The only level of management is upper management.		
9. A revenue center is a division or department that sells products that bring in money.		
10. Since support centers do not bring in any money, they are unimportant.		

Part 2

Look in the text to find support for each statement. If the text supports a statement, write *yes* in the *Text Supports?* column. Then write the text page number in the space below the statement. If the text does not support the statement, write *no* in the *Text Supports?* column. Then, in the space below the statement, rewrite the statement so that it is supported by the text.

Hospitality Terms Chapter 15

Name _____

Chapter 15

Date _____ Period _____

1									S											
2									O											
3									L											
4									E											
5									P											
6									R											
7									O											
8									P											
9									R											
10									I											
11									E											
12									T											
13									O											
14									R											
15									S											
16									H											
17									I											
18									P											

(continued)

Part 1

Use the clues below to fill in the missing words in the puzzle.

1. The right of partial ownership in a corporation.

2. The power to make decisions and to tell other workers what to do.

3. Making sure that a business accomplishes what it set out to accomplish.

4. A team of people who make decisions for the business.

5. The day-to-day running of a business.

6. The money a business takes in for the products and services it sells.

7. A business owned by one person.

8. A legal entity established for the purpose of doing business.

9. A form of ownership in which two or more people own the business.

10. Setting goals and developing methods to meet those goals.

11. A department that sells products that bring money into the business.

12. Shows how the tasks of the business are organized and who performs these tasks.

13. Designing the internal structure of the business.

14. A department that does not bring in money directly, but is necessary to the business.

15. A book that gives the details about how to run the business.

16. People who own stock in a corporation.

17. The money a business has left after all the costs of running the business are paid.

18. A record of the decisions made about goals and the methods to meet them.

(continued)

Part 2

Below are listed pairs of terms. On the lines below each pair of terms, explain the relationship of the two terms to each other.

19. sole proprietor *and* partners

_____

_____

_____

_____

20. manager *and* supervisor

_____

_____

_____

_____

21. owner-managed business *and* hired management

_____

_____

_____

_____

22. staffing *and* leading

_____

_____

_____

_____

23. upper management *and* middle management

_____

_____

_____

_____

24. supervisory management *and* reporting relationship

_____

_____

_____

_____

Ownership and Money

Activity C

Chapter 15

Name _____

Date _____ Period _____

Part 1: Ownership

The following terms are related to the ownership of businesses:

chain   franchise   sole proprietorship

corporation   partnership   stockholder

Choose a term from this list that best fills in each blank below.

_____ 1. John owns and runs the Southern Climates Bed & Breakfast him-self. John's business is a _____.

_____ 2. Colleen, Cathy, and Claire own the 3Cs Restaurant together. Their business is a _____.

_____ 3. The Bricks and Mortar Bakery is owned by stockholders. The Bricks and Mortar Bakery is a _____.

_____ 4. Imagine you own 120 shares of the Bricks and Mortar Bakery. You are a _____.

_____ 5. Colleen, Cathy, and Claire expand their business to three restau-rants. Their business is now a _____.

_____ 6. Shanita wants to open a unit of the 3Cs Restaurant. She asks Colleen, Cathy, and Claire if she can _____ a unit of their chain.

Part 2: Money

The following terms are related to the flow of money in businesses:

expenses   revenue   support center

profit   revenue center

Choose a term from this list that best fills in each blank below.

_____ 7. The rooms division of the hotel sells thousands of dollars of accommodations each month. The rooms division is a _____.

_____ 8. The money that the rooms division takes in is called either sales or _____.

_____ 9. The money that the business pays for salaries, supplies, and rent is called costs or _____.

_____ 10. The housekeeping department is a _____ because it prepares the rooms that the rooms division sells.

_____ 11. A business took in $150,000 in revenue. It paid out $148,000 in expenses. The $2,000 difference is the _____.

_____ 12. The beauty salon at the hotel is a _____ because it sells its services to guests.

Management

Name _____

Date _____ Period _____

The following terms are related to management:

controlling	middle management	planning
hired management	operations manual	reporting relationships
leading	organizational chart	staffing
manager	organizing	supervisory management
management	owner-managed	upper management

Choose a term from this list that best fills in the blanks below.

_____ 1. Crystal is the manager of a unit of a hotel chain. She reports to the regional manager. She supervises the managers in her hotel. Crystal is in _____ _____.

_____ 2. Joshua owns and operates his own business. He has three employees and supervises each of them. He has an _____-_____ business.

_____ 3. Antwone recently bought out a family owned restaurant, and he hired one of the former owners to run it. His business is run by _____ _____.

_____ 4. Tiffany is preparing to open her first ice cream shop. She is in the process of hiring and training workers. She is _____ her business.

_____ 5. Jacob, the new manager of a unit of a restaurant chain, consults the _____ _____ to learn how to run the restaurant.

_____ 6. Emma is the president of a large corporation. She is in _____ _____.

_____ 7. In order for Montel's business to grow, he needed to have procedures for _____ the business. These procedures would help him determine if the business was accomplishing his goals.

_____ 8. Jasmine was having trouble finding people to staff positions in _____ _____. These people must be experts at their work because they work directly with the workers in their departments.

_____ 9. Ricardo needed to develop a new _____ _____ for his company. The management team had reorganized the departments and reporting relationships.

_____ 10. Midori was _____ for the future of her business by setting goals and developing methods to meet those goals.

_____ 11. Michael was very good at _____ the people he worked with to accomplish his business goals. He motivated them, created a positive work atmosphere, and communicated well.

(continued)

_____ 12. Rachel just started a new job. She was unclear about which manager she should report to. She needs to learn about the _____ _____ in the company.

_____ 13. Evan's new job requires him to make decisions for the company. His job position is _____.

_____ 14. Shannon was having trouble _____ the business. She could not decide the best way to divide up the tasks to be done among the various divisions and departments.

_____ 15. Michelle put together a new _____ team to make decisions for the company.

Revisiting Chapter 15

Activity E

Name _____

Chapter 15

Date _____ Period _____

Write complete responses to each of the following questions and statements in the space provided.

1. The structure of a business is based on the following: _____

_____

_____

2. List two categories of business based on number of units. _____

_____

_____

3. List the three forms of business ownership. _____

_____

_____

4. Explain the difference between a sole proprietorship and a partnership. _____

_____

_____

5. Explain how a corporation is different from the other two forms of ownership. _____

_____

_____

_____

6. Explain the difference between an owner-managed business and hired management. _____

_____

_____

7. List the two types of multiple-unit businesses. _____

_____

8. Describe the similarities between a chain and a franchise. _____

_____

_____

_____

9. Describe the differences between a chain and a franchise. _____

_____

_____

_____

(continued)

Name

_____

10. List the five functions of management. _____
_____
_____

11. For each of the five functions you listed above, give an example from the hospitality industry.

A. _____
_____
_____

B. _____
_____
_____

C. _____
_____
_____

D. _____
_____
_____

E. _____
_____
_____

12. What does an organizational chart show? _____
_____
_____

13. List and describe the three levels of management. _____
_____
_____

14. Explain what a reporting relationship is and give an example. _____
_____
_____

15. Explain the difference between a revenue center and a support center. _____
_____
_____

16. Give two examples of a revenue center and two examples of a support center for a hotel. _____
_____
_____

Hospitality Management

Kick Off!

Activity A	Name _____
Chapter 16	Date _____ Period _____

Part 1

Read each statement below. Do you agree with the statement? Write *yes* or *no* in the *Agree?* column. Be ready to explain your reasons for each answer.

Statement	Agree?	Text Supports?
1. Hospitality management is not responsible for profitability.		
2. The general manager is the person responsible for the entire operation of a single unit of a hospitality business.		
3. Management responsibilities are never delegated.		
4. Hospitality managers are responsible for eight main tasks: goal setting, customer satisfaction, cost controls, record keeping, human resources, facility maintenance, sanitation and safety, and marketing.		
5. The management of human resources consists of four main tasks: hiring and training, supervising, planning shifts, and evaluating.		

(continued)

Statement	Agree?	Text Supports?
6. A supervisor is a manager who makes sure that employees do their jobs properly.		
7. The general manager of a food and beverage business or a lodging business is responsible for the health and safety of all guests and employees.		
8. There is one best type of management style for all situations.		
9. Managers are not interested in team spirit or motivating their employees.		
10. Hospitality managers need a variety of technical skills, but no computer skills.		

Part 2

Look in the text to find support for each statement. If the text supports a statement, write *yes* in the *Text Supports?* column. Then write the text page number in the space below the statement. If the text does not support the statement, write *no* in the *Text Supports?* column. Then, in the space below the statement, rewrite the statement so that it is supported by the text.

Hospitality Terms Chapter 16

Activity B

Chapter 16

Name _____

Date _____ Period _____

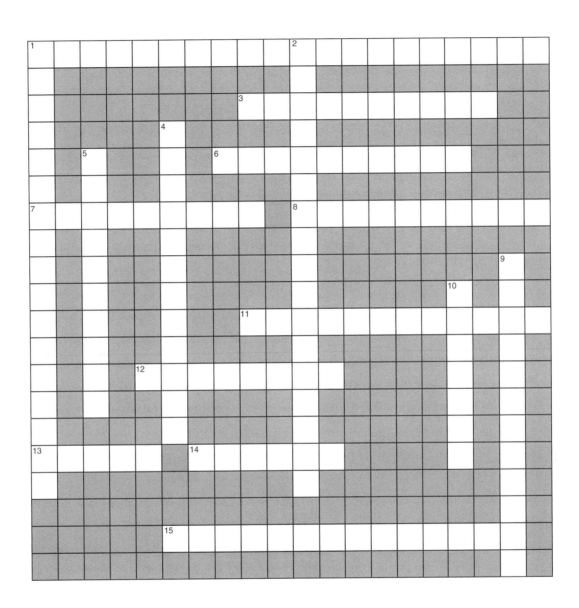

(continued)

Name

_____

Across

1. A formal review and evaluation of an employee's performance on the job is a _____ _____.

3. A _____ is a manager who makes sure that each employee does his or her job properly.

6. In the _____ management style, the manager shares the decision making with the employees.

7. A _____ worker willingly puts forth effort on the job.

8. An employee _____ is a formal review and evaluation of an employee's performance on the job.

11. In the _____ management style, the manager seeks employee input before he or she makes a final decision.

12. Another name for the general manager is the managing _____.

13. An _____-level worker has no previous experience in the business.

14. A _____ is a guideline for spending money.

15. A _____ _____ is a person hired to anonymously stay at a hotel or eat at a restaurant to observe and report on the quality.

Down

1. Another name for a performance appraisal is a _____ _____.

2. _____ _____ files contain information about each employee.

4. Skills in _____ will enable you to keep your tools and information in order.

5. In the _____ style of management, the supervisor gives orders to employees.

9. In the _____ leadership style, the employees make all the decisions.

10. The general _____ is responsible for the entire operation of a hospitality business.

Management Styles

Name _____

Date _____ Period _____

Management styles can be organized into four categories:

    autocratic style: the manager gives orders to the employees

    bureaucratic style: the manager seeks employees' input before he or she makes a final decision

    democratic style: the manger shares decision making with employees

    laissez-faire style: the manager lets the employees make all the decisions

For each example in Column A, write the type of style it illustrates in Column B. In Column C, give another example. The first one is done for you.

A. Example	B. Style	C. Your example
1. The manager tells the banquet crew to set up any way they choose.	laissez-faire	The crew asks the manager what setup he wants; he shrugs his shoulders and says, "It doesn't matter to me."
2. The manager gathered ideas from several employees and then decided what to do.		
3. The emergency coordinator announced, "You must do exactly as I say."		
4. The manager and team members talk through a problem and arrive at a group decision.		
5. "It's my way or the highway," is a key phrase of this manager.		
6. "Hearing your ideas will help me figure out how to make this work," is most likely to be said by this manager.		
7. "What do you think?" is a frequent question of this manager.		
8. When asked a question about the menu, the manager shrugged her shoulders and said, "Whatever."		
9. The manager insists on having the table set exactly as in the drawing.		

Hospitality Management

Name _____

Date _____ Period _____

Read each situation described below and respond to each request.

1. Imagine you have just been hired as the general manager of a newly remodeled hotel. The home office has told you to increase the average number of guests per night within three months. Which two of the eight management tasks will you need to address first? Why? _____

    _____

    _____

    _____

    _____

2. You have been invited to serve as a mystery shopper at a chain restaurant in your town. You are asked to eat there four times during the next month—once for breakfast, once for lunch, once for dinner, and one other time. After dining, you will complete a questionnaire and return it to the corporate office with your receipts. What are some questions you anticipate being asked on the questionnaire? _____

    _____

    _____

    _____

    _____

3. As the manager of a local restaurant, you notice that most of the customers are taking food home because they cannot eat the entire portion you serve. Others throw away approximately half of their food. What are some things you and your staff could study and consider in order to cut costs and increase profits? _____

    _____

    _____

    _____

    _____

4. As the executive housekeeper, you've been told a worker is transferring to your department from the foodservice department. You want to know more about the person. Where will you go and what will you review in order to get the information you need? What items will you most likely want to review? _____

    _____

    _____

    _____

    _____

Revisiting Chapter 16

Name _____

Date _____ Period _____

Part 1

Provide a complete answer for each of the following questions or statements in the space provided.

1. List four basic duties of the hospitality manager. _____

_____

_____

2. What is the title used for the person in charge of one unit of a hospitality business? _____

_____

3. What are the three methods by which managers control the costs of their businesses? _____

_____

_____

_____

4. A restaurant manager cuts the portion size of beef from 6 ounces to 4 ounces. This is an example of which method of cost control? _____

5. The inventory manager just instituted a new requisitioning system. Each employee must submit a form signed by his or her supervisor before an item is issued. This is an example of which method of cost control? _____

6. What is the key to successful hiring? _____

_____

7. What is the purpose of assigning supervisors to employees? _____

_____

8. What are the two parts of the performance review or performance appraisal? _____

_____

_____

9. Give an example of each of the following four styles of management.

   A. autocratic _____

   B. bureaucratic _____

   C. democratic _____

   D. laissez-faire _____

10. Compare and contrast *rewards* and *recognition*. _____

_____

_____

(continued)

_____

Part 2

Managers have eight main tasks. List these below in Column A. For each task, write a definition or description of the task in Column B and give an example of the task in Column C.

A. Tasks	B. Definition or description	C. Example
1.		
2.		
3.		
4.		
5.		
6.		
7.		
8.		

(continued)

Part 3

List the seven management skills in Column A. For each skill, write its definition or description in Column B and give an example of the skill in Column C.

A. Skills	B. Definition or description	C. Example
1.		
2.		
3.		
4.		
5.		
6.		
7.		

Human Resources

Kick Off!

Activity A

Chapter 17

Name _____

Date _____ Period _____

Part 1

Read each statement below. Do you agree with the statement? Write *yes* or *no* in the *Agree?* column. Be ready to explain your reasons for each answer.

Statement	Agree?	Text Supports?
1. Businesses use three types of resources: financial resources, capital resources, and human resources.		
2. When a company has a human resources division or department, the other managers do not perform any human resources tasks.		
3. A human resources department or division has the following eight major functions: recruitment, compensation and benefits, policies and procedures, regulatory compliance, employee performance, record keeping, labor relations, and employee retention.		
4. Recruitment includes placing ads in newspapers.		
5. Compensation refers only to the money paid to workers.		

(continued)

Statement	Agree?	Text Supports?
6. An employee handbook contains a company's policies and procedures.		
7. Three groups of laws affect human resources: equal opportunity, workers' rights, and safety laws.		
8. The human resources department is responsible for all training of all employees.		
9. Human resources departments do not need any computers for record keeping.		
10. Issues in human resources include diversity in the workforce, recruitment, family and medical leave, and quality of work life.		

Part 2

Look in the text to find support for each statement. If the text supports a statement, write *yes* in the *Text Supports?* column. Then write the text page number in the space below the statement. If the text does not support the statement, write *no* in the *Text Supports?* column. Then, in the space below the statement, rewrite the statement so that it is supported by the text.

Hospitality Terms Chapter 17

Activity B

Name _____

Chapter 17

Date _____ Period _____

Part 1

One way to learn about a term is to analyze it for words or word parts you already know. You will develop a term analysis for each term below. This term analysis has four parts: a. list of the words or parts of words in the term that you recognize, b. list of other terms that contain one or more of the words or word parts, c. definition based on this analysis, and d. the definition from the textbook. The first one is done for you.

1. human resources

    a. Write the words or word parts that you recognize.

    human, resource

    b. Write other terms you know that contain these words or word parts.

    humane, humanity, resourceful

    c. Write a definition based on your analysis of the words and word parts.

    resources provided by humans

    d. Write the definition from the textbook.

    people who work in a business

2. recruitment

    a. Write the words or word parts you recognize.

    _____

    b. Write other terms that you know that contain these words or word parts.

    _____

    c. Write a definition based on your analysis of the words and word parts.

    _____

    _____

    d. Write the definition from the textbook.

    _____

    _____

3. screening process

    a. Write the words or word parts you recognize.

    _____

    b. Write other terms that you know that contain these words or word parts.

    _____

(continued)

_____

c. Write a definition based on your analysis of the words and word parts.

_____

_____

d. Write the definition from the textbook.

_____

_____

4. compensation

a. Write the words or word parts you recognize.

_____

b. Write other terms that you know that contain these words or word parts.

_____

c. Write a definition based on your analysis of the words and word parts.

_____

_____

d. Write the definition from the textbook.

_____

_____

5. benefits

a. Write the words or word parts you recognize.

_____

b. Write other terms that you know that contain these words or word parts.

_____

c. Write a definition based on your analysis of the words and word parts.

_____

_____

d. Write the definition from the textbook.

_____

_____

6. discrimination

a. Write the words or word parts you recognize.

_____

b. Write other terms that you know that contain these words or word parts.

_____

(continued)

c. Write a definition based on your analysis of the words and word parts.

_____

_____

d. Write the definition from the textbook.

_____

_____

7. disability

   a. Write the words or word parts you recognize.

   _____

   b. Write other terms that you know that contain these words or word parts.

   _____

   c. Write a definition based on your analysis of the words and word parts.

   _____

   _____

   d. Write the definition from the textbook.

   _____

   _____

8. Americans with Disabilities Act

   a. Write the words or word parts you recognize.

   _____

   b. Write other terms that you know that contain these words or word parts.

   _____

   c. Write a definition based on your analysis of the words and word parts.

   _____

   _____

   d. Write the definition from the textbook.

   _____

   _____

9. minimum wage

   a. Write the words or word parts you recognize.

   _____

   b. Write other terms that you know that contain these words or word parts.

   _____

   c. Write a definition based on your analysis of the words and word parts.

   _____

   _____

(continued)

d. Write the definition from the textbook.

_____

_____

10. job description

a. Write the words or word parts you recognize.

_____

b. Write other terms that you know that contain these words or word parts.

_____

c. Write a definition based on your analysis of the words and word parts.

_____

_____

d. Write the definition from the textbook.

_____

_____

11. labor union

a. Write the words or word parts you recognize.

_____

b. Write other terms that you know that contain these words or word parts.

_____

c. Write a definition based on your analysis of the words and word parts.

_____

_____

d. Write the definition from the textbook.

_____

_____

12. turnover

a. Write the words or word parts you recognize.

_____

b. Write other terms that you know that contain these words or word parts.

_____

c. Write a definition based on your analysis of the words and word parts.

_____

_____

d. Write the definition from the textbook.

_____

_____

Job Scramble in Human Resources

Name _____

Date _____ Period _____

Unscramble the letters in the following phrases. Use the terms to compose a story about a worker in a hospitality business. Circle the 10 terms in your story.

_____ 1. nhaum sreescour

_____ 2. gnnieserc pcsroes

_____ 3. gewa

_____ 4. eeepmylo bkhdnaoo

_____ 5. dytisialbi

_____ 6. plyemeoe ttenernoi

_____ 7. orertnvu

_____ 8. nmmiium gaew

_____ 9. ojb tdrieiosncp

_____ 10. cmponseantoi

Once upon a time, _____

_____

_____

_____

_____

_____

_____

_____

_____

_____

_____

_____

_____

_____

_____

_____

_____

_____

Revisiting Chapter 17

Name _____

Date _____ Period _____

Read the following statements about human resources in hospitality. If the statement is true, write *T* in the blank. If the statement is false, rewrite the underlined portion of the statement to make it true.

_____ 1. Even in large businesses with human resources departments, managers are often still responsible for the following human resources tasks: <u>hiring, training, supervising, planning shifts, and evaluating.</u>

_____

_____

_____ 2. The typical way to advertise and recruit candidates for new positions is to <u>post job openings on the company Web site.</u>

_____

_____

_____ 3. HR performs screening of job candidates by <u>conducting formal interviews.</u>

_____

_____ 4. Preemployment drug testing is done by the <u>safety and sanitation</u> department.

_____

_____ 5. A person's <u>salary</u> consists of the money paid and the benefits provided to the person for his or her work.

_____

_____ 6. <u>Workers' compensation</u> laws require employers to provide medical and salary coverage for an illness or injury that an employee experiences as a result of the job.

_____

_____ 7. The purpose of policies and procedures is to ensure <u>that employees follow the rules closely.</u>

_____

_____ 8. <u>Personal harassment</u> is considered to be any unwelcome behavior of a sexual nature that creates an intimidating, hostile, or offensive work environment.

_____

_____ 9. Laws and regulations that affect human resources can be organized into three groups: <u>sexual harassment, employee retention, and workers' compensation.</u>

_____

_____

_____ 10. The purpose of the <u>Americans with Disabilities Act</u> is to ensure that people with disabilities are treated fairly in public places and in the workplace.

_____

(continued)

_____ 11. One of the most commonly known and recognized workers' rights is the <u>minimum wage</u>.

_____

_____ 12. If a tipped employee does not make enough in tips to meet the minimum wage, the employer <u>has no responsibility.</u>

_____

_____ 13. The major federal <u>sanitation</u> law is the Occupational Safety and Health Act (OSH Act).

_____

_____ 14. Managers and the human resources department usually work together to write <u>job descriptions</u> for each job.

_____

_____ 15. <u>Human worker files</u> should include the Social Security number, address, and phone number of each employee.

_____

_____ 16. Confidentiality is <u>essential</u> for human resources employees.

_____

_____ 17. A <u>labor union</u> is an organization formed to make sure that union members get fair wages, decent benefits, and safe working conditions.

_____

_____ 18. The term <u>turnover</u> describes what happens when an employee leaves the job to take a promotion, move out of town, or quits.

_____

_____ 19. Issues that often develop when people from different backgrounds or cultures work together include <u>prejudice, discrimination, sexual harassment, and communication problems</u>.

_____

_____

_____ 20. The <u>Quality of Work Life Act</u> was created to help workers deal with family needs and still keep their jobs.

_____

CHAPTER 18

Marketing and Sales

Kick Off!

Activity A

Chapter 18

Name _____

Date _____ Period _____

Part 1

Read each statement below. Do you agree with the statement? Write *yes* or *no* in the *Agree?* column. Be ready to explain your reasons for each answer.

Statement	Agree?	Text Supports?
1. Marketing has four major functions: learn what customers want and need, develop a product that meets those wants and needs, make sure that potential customers know about the product, and persuade customers to buy the product.		
2. Most of the products of the hospitality industry are goods.		
3. The five basic areas of marketing are target market, product, price, place, and promotion.		
4. The only definition of sales is promotion that occurs when a representative of the business speaks directly with a customer about a product.		
5. The development of brand identity is an important part of marketing.		

(continued)

Statement	Agree?	Text Supports?
6. The purpose of the marketing plan is to help the company accomplish its goals.		
7. A business does not need to know anything about similar businesses.		
8. The methods of promotion used in marketing are advertising, public relations, sales promotion, and personal selling.		
9. Hospitality businesses may use an outside marketing company.		
10. Nonprofit organizations and government groups may promote the hospitality industry.		

Part 2

Look in the text to find support for each statement. If the text supports a statement, write *yes* in the *Text Supports?* column. Then write the text page number in the space below the statement. If the text does not support the statement, write *no* in the *Text Supports?* column. Then, in the space below the statement, rewrite the statement so that it is supported by the text.

Hospitality Terms Chapter 18

Activity B

Name _____

Chapter 18

Date _____ Period _____

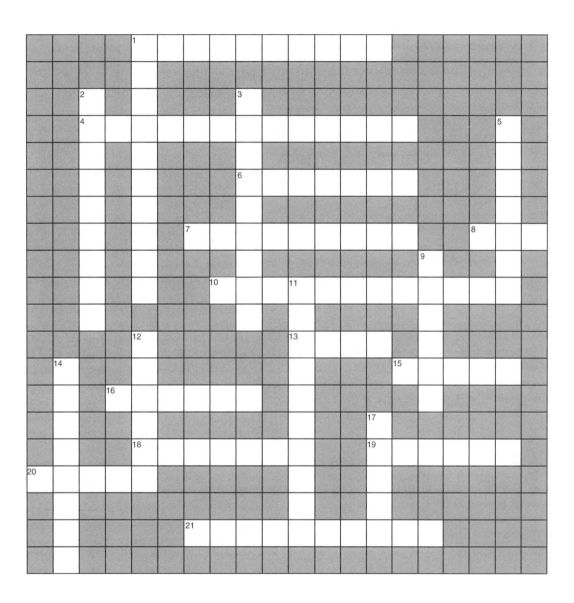

(continued)

Across

1. An advertisement broadcast on radio or television.

4. A single promotional advertising message.

6. A _____ program rewards frequent customers with free or lower-priced products.

7. Telling customers about a product or the company that offers the product with the purposes of persuading customers to buy the product and creating a positive image of the company and product.

8. The marketing _____ is the combination of decisions made about product, price, place, and promotion.

10. An article written by a company representative to use as the basis for news in a newspaper, radio, or TV news program.

13. Any product you can touch.

15. The type of promotion that occurs when a representative of the company speaks directly with a customer about a product.

16. Activities that are performed to create goodwill between the public and the business are called _____ relations.

18. Goods or services a business sells.

19. A _____ board is an announcement board located in a hotel lobby and other locations on a hotel property.

20. A _____ promotion is a specific offer designed to increase sales.

21. A business that wants to take away customers from a similar business.

Down

1. The _____ and visitors bureau is a nonprofit organization that promotes tourism and provides services to travelers.

2. Developing and promoting products that meet customer needs.

3. A type of print advertising that appears on a large, outdoor panel.

5. An activity done for another person.

9. Satisfied customers who return again and again to a business are called _____ customers.

11. Recommending additional products or services to a customer while the customer is buying something else is called _____ selling.

12. Product, price, place, and promotion are the _____ _____ of marketing.

14. Finding out about the market and potential customers for a business is called marketing _____.

17. Promotional messages that appear on paper, such as in newspapers and magazines, are called _____ advertising.

Analyzing Marketing Terms

Activity C

Name _____

Chapter 18

Date _____ Period _____

One way to learn about a term is to analyze it for words or word parts you already know. You will develop a term analysis for each term below. The term analysis has four parts: a. list of the words or parts of words in the term you recognize, b. list of other terms that contain one or more of the words or word parts, c. definition based on this analysis, and d. the definition from the textbook. The first one is done for you.

1. market segmentation

    a. Write the words or word parts that you recognize.

    market, segment

    b. Write other terms you know that contain these words or word parts.

    marketing, supermarket, farmer's market

    c. Write a definition based on your analysis of the words and word parts.

    a part of the market

    d. Write the definition from the textbook.

    the process of dividing a large market into segments

2. revenue management software

    a. Write the words or word parts that you recognize.

    _____

    b. Write other terms you know that contain these words or word parts.

    _____

    c. Write a definition based on your analysis of the words and word parts.

    _____

    _____

    d. Write the definition from the textbook.

    _____

    _____

3. personal communication

    a. Write the words or word parts that you recognize.

    _____

    b. Write other terms you know that contain these words or word parts.

    _____

    c. Write a definition based on your analysis of the words and word parts.

    _____

    _____

(continued)

d. Write the definition from the textbook.

_____

_____

4. nonpersonal communication

   a. Write the words or word parts that you recognize.

   _____

   b. Write other terms you know that contain these words or word parts.

   _____

   c. Write a definition based on your analysis of the words and word parts.

   _____

   _____

   d. Write the definition from the textbook.

   _____

   _____

5. marketing plan

   a. Write the words or word parts that you recognize.

   _____

   b. Write other terms you know that contain these words or word parts.

   _____

   c. Write a definition based on your analysis of the words and word parts.

   _____

   _____

   d. Write the definition from the textbook.

   _____

   _____

6. advertising

   a. Write the words or word parts that you recognize.

   _____

   b. Write other terms you know that contain these words or word parts.

   _____

   c. Write a definition based on your analysis of the words and word parts.

   _____

   _____

(continued)

    d. Write the definition from the textbook.

_____

_____

7. Internet advertising

    a. Write the words or word parts that you recognize.

_____

    b. Write other terms you know that contain these words or word parts.

_____

    c. Write a definition based on your analysis of the words and word parts.

_____

_____

    d. Write the definition from the textbook.

_____

_____

8. publicity

    a. Write the words or word parts that you recognize.

_____

    b. Write other terms you know that contain these words or word parts.

_____

    c. Write a definition based on your analysis of the words and word parts.

_____

_____

    d. Write the definition from the textbook.

_____

_____

Marketing and Sales

Name _____

Date _____ Period _____

Write a complete response to the following questions and statements in the space provided.

1. Define the two types of products and give a hospitality example of each.

   good: _____

   _____

   service: _____

   _____

2. Describe marketing research and market segmentation. _____

   _____

   _____

3. List the four Ps of marketing and give an example of each. _____

   _____

   _____

   _____

4. Explain the purpose of revenue management software. _____

   _____

5. In your own words, describe the difference between personal communication and nonpersonal communication. Give a hospitality example of each. _____

   _____

   _____

   _____

   _____

6. List at least three advantages to competition._____

   _____

   _____

   _____

   _____

7. In your own words, describe the difference between advertising and public relations. _____

   _____

   _____

8. What are three advantages for hospitality businesses when government and nonprofit organizations promote the hospitality industry? _____

   _____

   _____

Revisiting Chapter 18

Activity E   Name _____

Chapter 18   Date _____ Period _____

Read each statement below. Fill in the letters for the missing words. Then either complete the statement or answer the question.

1. Developing products that meet customer needs and promoting those products so customers will buy them is <u>m</u> _ _ _ _ _ _ _ _ _. Describe two hospitality products that a hospitality marketer might develop. _____

    _____

2. By using market <u>s</u> _ _ _ _ _ _ _ _ _ _ _ _, a business is able to identify its target market. What are the four characteristics of a good target market? _____

    _____

3. The four Ps of marketing can be combined in various ways to create a <u>m</u> _ _ _ _ _ _ _ _ _ <u>m</u> _ _. The four Ps are _____

    _____

4. There are four types of <u>p</u> _ _ _ _ _ _ _ _ _ used to communicate with customers. They are _____

    _____

    _____

5. Brand <u>i</u> _ _ _ _ _ _ _ should represent all the decisions made about the target market, product, price, place, and promotion. Name the three elements that make up a brand. _____

    _____

    _____

6. Management of a hospitality business will use marketing research and sales data to develop the <u>m</u> _ _ _ _ _ _ _ _ _ <u>p</u> _ _ _. Its purpose is to _____

    _____

7. Businesses who want to take away your customers are called your <u>c</u> _ _ _ _ _ _ _ _ _ _ _. Why do you need to know about these businesses? _____

    _____

8. Marketing and upper management work together to develop specific <u>g</u> _ _ _ _. Give an example of this related to hospitality. _____

    _____

(continued)

9. A promotional message about a product that is paid for by a sponsor is called an
a <u> </u> _ _ _ _ _ _ _ _ _ _ _ _. Four of the most common forms are _____
_____

10. A synonym for broadcast advertising is <u>c</u> _ _ _ _ _ _ _ _ _ _. To produce broadcast
advertising, you need _____
_____

11. A <u>r</u> _ _ _ _ _ _ <u>b</u> _ _ _ _ is an announcement in a hotel lobby or other location at the
lodging property. Whether on a board or TV, it typically lists _____
_____

12. Activities performed to create a positive feeling or feeling of approval between the public and
the business are known as <u>p</u> _ _ _ _ _ _ <u>r</u> _ _ _ _ _ _ _ _ _. The two parts of it are
_____
_____

13. In marketing, an incentive is usually called a <u>s</u> _ _ _ _ _ <u>p</u> _ _ _ _ _ _ _ _ _. Three
examples of this are _____
_____

14. When a salesperson recommends additional products to the customer, this is
<u>s</u> _ _ _ _ _ _ _ _ _ _ <u>s</u> _ _ _ _ _ _. Three examples of items a restaurant server
might recommend include the following: _____
_____

15. Hospitality businesses need sales representatives for g _ _ _ _ _ s _ _ _ _ _. List three
qualities these sales representatives need. _____
_____

16. Some companies specialize in specific areas of <u>m</u> _ _ _ _ _ _ _ _ _. Three examples are
_____
_____

17. The public relations manager of a single-unit <u>l</u> _ _ _ _ _ _ <u>p</u> _ _ _ _ _ _ _ is
responsible for these three tasks: _____
_____

(continued)

18. A major advantage of a chain is more r __ __ __ __ __ __ __ __ for marketing. What does the marketing department for a chain usually do?_____

_____

19. Many government and nonprofit o __ __ __ __ __ __ __ __ __ __ __ __ promote the hospitality industry. Three levels of these organizations are _____

_____

20. Many cities and regions have a CVB, which is the acronym for c __ __ __ __ __ __ __ __ __ and
v __ __ __ __ __ __ __ b __ __ __ __ __ . A CVB is _____

_____

● Accounting

Kick Off!

Activity A	Name _____
Chapter 19	Date _____ Period _____

Part 1

Read each statement below. Do you agree with the statement? Write *yes* or *no* in the *Agree?* column. Be ready to explain your reasons for each answer.

Statement	Agree?	Text Supports?
1. Accounting is a system of recording and summarizing financial transactions and then analyzing and reporting the results.		
2. A credit is added; a debit is subtracted.		
3. Accounting departments have five main functions: keep track of all financial transactions, categorize transactions, make payments and deposits, control costs, and prepare financial reports and statements.		
4. Most hospitality businesses name and organize their accounts in any way they please.		
5. The top manager in an accounting department is called the chief accountant.		

(continued)

Statement	Agree?	Text Supports?
6. The accounting division in a large hotel is usually divided into five departments: accounts receivable, accounts payable, night audit, credit, and food and beverage controller.		
7. Accounts payable consists of money that a hospitality business owes to other businesses.		
8. Employees in accounting departments must pay attention to detail.		
9. Employees in the accounting department do not need to have a good working relationship with employees in the front office.		
10. Computer systems, such as the PMS and POS, have reduced the workload in the accounting department.		

Part 2

Look in the text to find support for each statement. If the text supports a statement, write *yes* in the *Text Supports?* column. Then write the text page number in the space below the statement. If the text does not support the statement, write *no* in the *Text Supports?* column. Then, in the space below the statement, rewrite the statement so that it is supported by the text.

Hospitality Terms Chapter 19

Activity B

Activity B

Name _____

Chapter 19

Date _____ Period _____

Part 1

Match each term below to its definition. Write the term in the blank in front of its definition.

_____ 1. The process of buying something and paying for it.

_____ 2. Money paid to employees for their labor.

_____ 3. Money that is owed or taken out of a business; money subtracted from the total.

_____ 4. Money paid to the federal, state, and local government required by law.

_____ 5. Financial record that lists transactions and shows the balance.

_____ 6. Money that is owed to the business.

_____ 7. Money that a business owes to other businesses.

_____ 8. A careful examination of the financial records of a person or company.

_____ 9. Careful examination of a hotel's financial transactions for the day.

_____ 10. Entering room charges into the guest folio.

_____ 11. The department whose goal it is to protect the business from loss due to customers or businesses with bad credit.

_____ 12. The top manager of an accounting department or division.

account

accounts payable

accounts receivable

audit

controller

credit department

debit

financial transaction

income statement

night audit

payroll

posting charges

taxes

(continued)

Name

_____

Part 2

Match each term below to its definition. Write the term in the blank in front of its definition.

_____ 13. A book in which each financial transaction is recorded.

_____ 14. A system of recording and summarizing financial transactions and then analyzing and reporting the results.

_____ 15. Money or payment that has been received; money added to the total.

_____ 16. An organized way of naming and categorizing accounts.

_____ 17. The system that provides uniform names for each category of account for use throughout the hospitality industry; makes it possible to compare financial data.

_____ 18. The worker who collects money that is owed to a business.

_____ 19. The worker who pays invoices that a business owes to other businesses.

_____ 20. The person who carefully examines a hotel's financial transactions for that day, at the end of the day.

_____ 21. A record that shows whether a person or business pays its bills promptly.

_____ 22. The accountant for the food and beverage department of a hotel.

_____ 23. People who are late with payments they owe a hotel.

_____ 24. Place where goods or services are sold and money is collected.

accounting

accounts payable clerk

accounts receivable clerk

balance sheet

credit

credit history

delinquent guests

food and beverage controller

ledger

night auditor

point of sale

system of accounts

Uniform System of Accounts

(continued)

Part 3

Each of the following pairs of terms has words in common. However, each term has its own meaning. For each pair below, explain the difference between the two terms.

25. accounts receivable *and* accounts receivable clerk

_____

_____

_____

26. accounts payable *and* accounts payable clerk

_____

_____

_____

27. audit *and* night audit

_____

_____

_____

28. credit department *and* credit history

_____

_____

_____

Accounting

Read each of the following hospitality accounting situations carefully. Then write a complete response to each question or statement in the space provided. Base your answers on the information provided in Chapter 19.

1. Jason has been asked to figure out how much money his company is making. What three reports or statements would he use to gather the data he needs to answer this question? _____

   _____

   _____

2. Ariana works in the controller's office for a large restaurant chain. With which three responsibilities will she likely assist? _____

   _____

   _____

3. Tia is in training for her new job in the accounts payable office. As part of her training, she has to follow an invoice from the time it arrives in the department until it is paid. List the steps she will follow. _____

   _____

   _____

   _____

4. Roseanne works as an auditor for a private company. When she comes to audit your hotel, what will be her two primary jobs? _____

   _____

   _____

   _____

5. The Green Hat Society has asked to hold a workshop at your hotel. Your credit department alerts you to have this group pay all expenses up front in cash upon making the reservation. What actions did the credit department probably take that led to this recommendation? _____

   _____

   _____

   _____

6. Dominique is preparing to fill an opening in his accounting department. Write two questions he can ask all the applicants he interviews to find out about their personal qualities and skills.

   _____

   _____

   _____

   _____

Personal Qualities and Skills

Name _____

Date _____ Period _____

Column A lists some personal qualities and skills needed for accounting work. In Column B, write an example of an action that would support that quality or skill. Use Column C to write a statement or question a person with this quality or skill might use. The first one is done for you.

A. Qualities/Skills	B. Supportive Action	C. Statement
1. Honesty	Customer gives too much money to cashier. Cashier returns amount overpaid.	"It wouldn't be right to keep the extra money."
2. Integrity		
3. Persistence		
4. Attention to detail		
5. Positive attitude		
6. Business accounting knowledge		
7. Problem-solving skills		
8. Customer relations skills		

Revisiting Chapter 19

Provide a complete response to each of the following questions or statements.

1. Explain how credits and debits differ._____

   _____

   _____

2. List the five main functions of accounting departments. _____

   _____

   _____

   _____

   _____

3. List four types of transactions hospitality businesses must track. _____

   _____

   _____

   _____

   _____

4. What is a guest folio? _____

   _____

   _____

   _____

5. How are separate accounts used in an accounting system? _____

   _____

   _____

6. How does the Uniform System of Accounts help large hospitality businesses? _____

   _____

   _____

7. Imagine that you work in the accounting department of a hotel. You notice that the cost of shampoo for the hotel rooms has suddenly gone up. What should you do based on this information? _____

   _____

   _____

   _____

(continued)

8. Describe the three basic financial statements of the accounting department. _____

_____

_____

_____

9. What is the title of the person in charge of the accounting department, and what are this employee's responsibilities? _____

_____

_____

_____

10. What is the difference in the responsibilities of the accounts receivable department and the accounts payable department? _____

_____

_____

_____

11. What are the purposes of an audit? _____

_____

_____

_____

12. What are three responsibilities of the night auditor? _____

_____

_____

_____

13. Imagine that you are the treasurer of the local Birding Club. The club meets once a week at a restaurant for lunch, and you pay the bill for the meal from the member dues. You would like to start an account with the restaurant. What would the advantages of this arrangement be for the Birding Club? for the restaurant?

_____

_____

_____

_____

_____

14. Before the restaurant will approve a credit account for the Birding Club, what will they check?

_____

_____

(continued)

15. Imagine that you are in charge of accounting for the food and beverage department in a large hotel. What is your title?

_____

_____

16. Sid is a salesman who frequently stays at your hotel and has an account with you. He consistently paid for the first three months, but the due date for the fourth month has passed and he has not paid. Sid would be referred to as a _____

_____

17. Ling sees Sid arriving at the hotel to check in. She knows he is late on his payment. How should this affect her attitude toward him, and why? _____

_____

_____

_____

18. What are the two most important personal qualities of employees who deal with money? _____

_____

_____

19. List two types of technological innovations that have greatly reduced the workload for hospitality accounting departments. _____

_____

_____

_____

20. In a large hotel, which department performs many financial tasks and works closely with the accounting department? _____

_____

Workplace Safety and Emergencies

Kick Off!

Activity A

Chapter 20

Name _____

Date _____ Period _____

Part 1

Read each statement below. Do you agree with the statement? Write *yes* or *no* in the *Agree?* column. Be ready to explain your reasons for each answer.

Statement	Agree?	Text Supports?
1. The Occupational Safety and Health Act requires employers to make the workplace free of hazards that might cause injury or death to employees.		
2. The four main causes of accidents are a poor accident prevention plan, employee lack of knowledge and skills, employee negligence, and employee fatigue.		
3. There is nothing employees can do to prevent accidents.		
4. An emergency action plan is a general description of what to do to prevent accidents.		
5. In most emergencies, a hospitality worker should call 9-1-1 immediately.		

(continued)

Statement	Agree?	Text Supports?
6. The evacuation plan for a facility should include instructions for meeting the special needs of people who cannot see or hear, as well as those who have mobility problems.		
7. When you cannot tell if an accident that has occurred is major or minor, you should assume it is minor.		
8. Fire needs fuel, carbon dioxide, and heat in order to burn.		
9. Every hospitality employee should know how to treat a minor injury.		
10. If you are not trained in first aid, there is nothing you can do during a medical emergency.		

Part 2

Look in the text to find support for each statement. If the text supports a statement, write *yes* in the *Text Supports?* column. Then write the text page number in the space below the statement. If the text does not support the statement, write *no* in the *Text Supports?* column. Then, in the space below the statement, rewrite the statement so that it is supported by the text.

Hospitality Terms Chapter 20

Activity B

Name _____

Chapter 20

Date _____ Period _____

Match each term below to its definition. Write the term in the blank in front of its definition.

ABC extinguisher
abdominal thrust
accident
combustible
compliance
CPR
emergency
emergency action plan
emergency coordinator
emergency medical services
emergency medical technician

emergency procedures
evacuation
fatigue
fire extinguisher
fire triangle
first aid
flammable liquid
hazard
major emergency
material safety data sheet
minor emergency
minor injury

negligence
Occupational Safety and Health Act
Occupational Safety and Health Administration
paramedic
right-to-know
safety
safety procedures

_____ 1. An unforeseen event that can cause harm to people and property.

_____ 2. The federal agency responsible for making sure the laws and regulations of the OSH Act are followed.

_____ 3. The requirement that employers must inform employees about any toxic or dangerous materials used in the workplace.

_____ 4. The person given the authority to make decisions during emergencies.

_____ 5. An emergency that does not require the help of an expert.

_____ 6. The three items a fire needs to keep burning: fuel, oxygen, and heat.

_____ 7. Emergency medical professionals and medical equipment, which are brought to the scene in an ambulance.

_____ 8. A first aid procedure designed to force a stuck object out of the throat.

_____ 9. Easy to burn.

_____ 10. A medical professional trained and licensed to perform emergency medical care.

_____ 11. The law that requires employers to make the workplace free of hazards that might cause injury or death to employees.

_____ 12. Procedures that include everything done to respond to an emergency that has already occurred.

(continued)

_____ 13. A detailed, usually written, plan that describes what to do in case of an emergency.

_____ 14. Procedures that include everything done to prevent an accident or emergency.

_____ 15. An unexpected event caused by carelessness or ignorance that results in harm to people or property.

_____ 16. The following of rules and policies.

_____ 17. Tiredness that can be caused by physical exertion, stress, or lack of sleep.

_____ 18. The orderly movement of people out of a dangerous location.

_____ 19. A type of fire extinguisher that can safely be used on Class A, B, and C fires.

_____ 20. A situation that could result in an accident or emergency.

_____ 21. Behaviors such as carelessness, laziness, ignoring the rules, and improper use of equipment.

_____ 22. An emergency that is life-threatening or requires professional help.

_____ 23. A container filled with materials that will put out a fire.

_____ 24. A form completed by a manufacturer for each hazardous substance it makes.

_____ 25. A liquid that catches fire easily and burns quickly.

_____ 26. A first aid procedure to help someone whose heart has stopped beating.

_____ 27. The treatment given to an injured or suddenly ill person before professional medical care arrives.

_____ 28. The actions taken to prevent accidents and emergencies.

_____ 29. Another name for a paramedic.

_____ 30. An injury that does *not* require the help of an expert.

Emergencies in the Workplace

Activity C   Name _____

Chapter 20   Date _____ Period _____

Write complete answers to each of the following questions and statements in the space provided.

1. What is the main purpose of the Occupational Health and Safety Act? _____

   _____

   _____

2. List the four causes of accidents in the workplace. _____

   _____

   _____

   _____

   _____

3. List and describe the three parts of an accident prevention program. _____

   _____

   _____

   _____

4. List three ways employees can prevent accidents. _____

   _____

   _____

   _____

5. What is the purpose of an emergency action plan? _____

   _____

   _____

6. Give an example of a minor emergency and a major emergency, and explain why they are classified as such. _____

   _____

   _____

   _____

   _____

7. Explain the fire triangle. _____

   _____

   _____

   _____

(continued)

8. List the 10 steps of a general emergency procedure. _____

_____

_____

_____

_____

_____

_____

_____

_____

_____

9. List the six do's while waiting for medical help. _____

_____

_____

_____

_____

_____

_____

10. List the five don'ts while waiting for medical help. _____

_____

_____

_____

_____

_____

Revisiting Chapter 20

Activity D   Name _____

Chapter 20   Date _____ Period _____

Write complete responses to the following questions and statements in the space provided.

1. Explain the difference between the terms *safety* and *emergency*. _____

   _____

   _____

   _____

2. What role does the federal government play in safety in the workplace?_____

   _____

   _____

   _____

3. List the three areas in which state and local governments make safety regulations._____

   _____

   _____

   _____

4. Which two causes of accidents are responsibilities of the employer, and which two are responsibilities of the employee?

   employer: _____

   _____

   employee: _____

   _____

5. How often should rules and policies be reviewed and updated? _____

   _____

6. What is the purpose of the right-to-know requirement of the OSH Act? _____

   _____

   _____

7. Imagine that you are a new server at a local restaurant. According to OSHA, you have responsibilities for workplace health and safety. What are they? _____

   _____

   _____

   _____

   _____

   _____

(continued)

8. What are the minimum six areas that an emergency action plan should cover? _____

_____

_____

_____

_____

_____

9. Imagine that you are serving as the emergency coordinator for your facility. What responsibilities will you have during an emergency? _____

_____

_____

_____

_____

10. What are the six elements of an evacuation plan? _____

_____

_____

_____

_____

_____

11. Who should engage in rescue work and emergency medical care? Why? _____

_____

12. Why should you call for help when you cannot tell if an injury is minor or major? _____

_____

13. Imagine that you discover the oil in the French fry machine is overheating to the point that it
might catch fire. What part of the fire triangle can you most quickly and safely remove? What
action should you take to do this? _____

_____

_____

_____

(continued)

14. List the four classes of fires and tell what types of materials are burning in each type.

_____

_____

_____

_____

15. In most companies, what is the first step an employee should take if he or she realizes an emergency is occurring? _____

_____

16. List three kinds of major emergencies. _____

_____

_____

_____

17. What is the purpose of practice drills, such as fire drills and tornado drills?_____

_____

_____

_____

18. If you are not certified in CPR or do not recall how to do it, should you try to perform CPR in an emergency? Why or why not? _____

_____

_____

_____

_____

19. List five weather conditions that can cause emergencies. _____

_____

_____

_____

_____

_____

20. Imagine that you are a server at a restaurant, and you are trained in the abdominal thrust (first aid technique). You notice a customer who seems to be choking. What signals indicate that a person is choking? _____

_____

_____

_____

Legal and Ethical Considerations

Kick Off!

Activity A	Name _____
Chapter 21	Date _____ Period _____

Part 1

Read each statement below. Write *yes* or *no* in the *Agree?* column. Be ready to explain your reasons for each answer.

Statement	Agree?	Text Supports?
1. Ethical behavior is going along with the crowd and doing whatever you are pressured to do.		
2. Laws affecting the hospitality industry include laws about hiring and employment, worker safety, food safety, building and zoning, environmental protection, smoking ordinances, and liquor laws.		
3. Licenses and permits are two of the main ways that agencies enforce governmental regulations.		
4. Hospitality businesses have liability issues in four areas: guest injuries, damage to property, theft of property, and guest privacy.		
5. According to common law, rights of guests include decent and humane treatment and total use of the room.		

(continued)

Statement	Agree?	Text Supports?
6. Innkeepers have the right to enter a guest's room for cleaning and maintenance.		
7. Unethical behavior is often illegal.		
8. Ethical qualities include honesty, integrity, trustworthiness, loyalty, fairness, concern for others, commitment to excellence, and accountability.		
9. Ethical behavior is not important in hospitality businesses.		
10. A good work ethic is an attitude that combines average work, average performance, and average results.		

Part 2

Look in the text to find support for each statement. If the text supports a statement, write *yes* in the *Text Supports?* column. Then write the text page number in the space below the statement. If the text does not support the statement, write *no* in the *Text Supports?* column. Then, in the space below the statement, rewrite the statement so that it is supported by the text.

Hospitality Terms Chapter 21

Activity B

Activity B   Name _____

Chapter 21   Date _____ Period _____

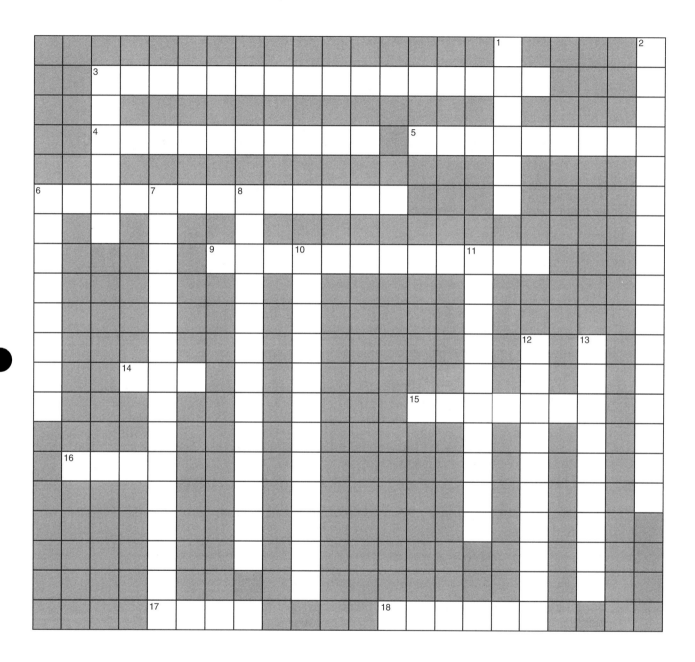

(continued)

Name

_____

Across

3. Process by which the employer subtracts taxes from each employee's paycheck and sends the taxes directly to the appropriate government agency.

4. A specific rule that is developed based on a law.

5. A regulation made by a local government.

6. Rules and regulations designed to make buildings safe.

9. A written list of rules for ethical behavior.

14. Acronym for the government agency that makes and enforces regulations based on the Food, Drug, and Cosmetic Act.

15. A document that gives the holder permission to do something.

16. Society's rules for proper behavior.

17. A list of regulations.

18. A system of moral rules that help people decide right from wrong.

Down

1. The process of designating specific geographic areas for specific uses.

2. A department of government that is responsible for enforcing a law.

3. Written permission to do something.

6. Doing the right thing, even when under pressure to do the wrong thing, is known as ethical _____.

7. The Food, _____, _____ _____ Act is the law that requires that food, drugs, and cosmetics sold to the public to be proven safe and effective.

8. An attitude that combines hard work, good performance, and dependable results.

10. A type of stealing that occurs when a trusted employee takes either goods or money entrusted to him or her.

11. A formal visit for the purpose of making sure that regulations are being followed.

12. Laws that list geographic areas and state the permitted uses for each area.

13. Doing the wrong thing is known as _____ behavior.

Legal and Ethical Considerations

Activity C

Chapter 21

Name _____

Date _____ Period _____

Read the following statements about legal and ethical considerations in hospitality businesses. If the statement is true, write a *T* in the blank before the statement. If the statement is false, rewrite the underlined portion of the statement to make it true.

_____ 1. Laws have been developed to protect customers, workers, the environment, and business owners <u>against ethical practices</u>.

_____

_____ 2. Rules and regulations made by the <u>federal government</u> are often called *ordinances*.

_____

_____ 3. A list of regulations is called an <u>ordinance</u>.

_____

_____ 4. <u>Workers' rights laws</u> require employers to treat everyone equally during the hiring process.

_____

_____ 5. The main way national, state, and local governments collect taxes is by <u>donation</u>.

_____

_____ 6. <u>Social Security</u> is a federal program that ensures that all workers will get some income after they retire.

_____

_____ 7. The Food, Drug, and Cosmetic Act requires that food, drugs, and cosmetics sold to the public <u>must be safe and effective</u>.

_____

_____ 8. <u>Commercial zones</u> are for businesses that are heavy, such as mining and power plants.

_____

_____ 9. Hospitality industries are usually in <u>industrial zones</u>.

_____

_____ 10. The role of the <u>zoning board</u> is to enforce the zoning laws of a community.

_____

_____ 11. Building inspectors <u>evaluate suggestions and vote on building codes</u>.

_____

_____ 12. The Environmental Protection Agency (EPA) is responsible for <u>setting smoking ordinances</u>.

_____

(continued)

_____ 13. Fines against smoking on airplanes are severe because of <u>the airlines' prejudice against smokers</u>.

_____ 14. Two main ways that governmental agencies enforce regulations are through <u>licensing and inspections</u>.

_____ 15. A <u>liquor license</u> is usually required of all places that sell liquor.

_____ 16. A <u>license</u> is a document that gives the holder permission to do something.

_____ 17. In order to conduct a workplace inspection, OSHA officials <u>must notify a business they are coming during a given week</u>.

_____ 18. Making sure restaurants and health care agencies follow health and safety regulations is the responsibility of <u>the USDA</u>.

_____ 19. Innkeepers have the right to enter guest rooms <u>at any time and for any reason</u>.

_____ 20. Hotels purchase <u>insurance policies</u> to protect themselves from a variety of risks.

_____ 21. Safe deposit boxes are offered in many hotels to protect the hotel <u>from liability for theft</u>.

_____ 22. Guest room numbers <u>may be given</u> to callers who inquire about guests.

_____ 23. In many cultures, the <u>basic rule of ethics</u> is the Golden Rule: Do unto others as you would have them do unto you.

_____ 24. Truth-in-menu laws have been developed to protect customers <u>from ethical restaurant owners</u>.

_____ 25. Acting in a professional manner shows your manager and coworkers you are <u>trustworthy and dependable</u>.

Qualities for Ethical Behavior

Activity D

Chapter 21

Name _____

Date _____ Period _____

Your textbook described eight qualities for ethical behavior. List these qualities in Column A of the chart below. Use Column B to give an example of an action that shows the quality. In Column C, write a statement or question the person might use that would be evidence of the quality. The first one has been done for you.

A. Qualities	B. Supportive Action	C. Statement
1. Honesty	Room attendant finds a diamond ring in a just vacated room, and turns the ring over to security.	"It would not be right to keep someone else's ring."
2.		
3.		
4.		
5.		
6.		
7.		
8.		

Revisiting Chapter 21

Name _____

Date _____ Period _____

Read each statement below. Fill in the letters for the missing words. Then either complete the statement or answer the question.

1. Society's rules for proper behavior are called l __ __ __. In the United States, society makes these rules through these three levels of government:

   _____

   _____

2. A r __ __ __ __ __ __ __ __ __ is a specific rule that is developed based on a law. These rules are needed because _____

   _____

3. Laws that affect the h __ __ __ __ __ __ __ __ __ __ __ industry can be grouped into the following seven categories:

   _____

   _____

   _____

   _____

4. Many laws have been developed to protect workers during hiring and during e __ __ __ __ __ __ __ __ __ __. They can be grouped into the following three areas: _____

   _____

   _____

5. Employers collect taxes for the government by taking money from a worker's pay through p __ __ __ __ __ __ d __ __ __ __ __ __ __ __ __. What national law governs income taxes? _____

   _____

6. The Occupational Safety and Health Act is the main f __ __ __ __ __ __ law that protects the safety of the worker. The Act also established the _____

   _____

7. The USDA monitors the s __ __ __ __ __ of these three products: _____

   _____

(continued)

Name

_____

8. The safety and wholesomeness of all other food is monitored by the F __ __ __   a __ __
   D __ __ __   A __ __ __ __ __ __ __ __ __ __ __ __ __ __ __. Other things they monitor include

   _____

9. Cities and counties are often z __ __ __ __ according to the following four types of land use:

   _____

10. If you want to build a new hospitality business, you will have to get approval from a
    z __ __ __ __ __ __   b __ __ __ __. Its role is _____

    _____

11. Each community has its own set of b __ __ __ __ __ __ __ __   c __ __ __ __ __. Their purpose is to

    _____

12. The quality of the e __ __ __ __ __ __ __ __ __ __ __ impacts the hospitality industry in the follow-
    ing two ways: _____

    _____

13. Because of medical research, efforts have been made to eliminate s __ __ __ __ __ __ in public
    places. Four places that it has been banned are _____

    _____

14. Two main ways that g __ __ __ __ __ __ __ __ __   a __ __ __ __ __ __ __ enforce government
    regulations are through licenses and inspections. The difference between these two is _____

    _____

    _____

15. Three agencies that conduct i __ __ __ __ __ __ __ __ __ __ __ are _____

    _____

16. Hospitality businesses have special l __ __ __ __ __   o __ __ __ __ __ __ __ __ __ __ __ to their guests
    in the following areas:_____

    _____

17. The three types of i __ __ __ __ __ __ __ __ __ that hotels purchase include _____

    _____

18. A system that helps people decide right from wrong is known as e __ __ __ __ __ __. What kind of
    behavior does this system encourage?_____

    _____

(continued)

19. U __ __ __ __ __ __ __ behavior is often illegal. Give an example of this type of behavior.

_____

_____

20. Truth-in-menu laws have been developed to protect c __ __ __ __ __ __ __ __ from unethical restaurant owners. In what two ways could a menu be untrue?_____

_____

21. A c __ __ __ of e __ __ __ __ __ is a written list of rules for ethical behavior. What kinds of groups have these lists?_____

_____

22. It is both illegal and unethical to d __ __ __ __ __ __ __ __ __ __ __ against another person. On what basis do people often discriminate? _____

_____

23. Hard work, good performance, and dependable results are a part of a g __ __ __ w __ __ __ e __ __ __ __. Four guidelines to using this are _____

_____

_____

_____

_____

24. New types of t __ __ __ __ __ __ __ __ __ have caused companies to watch out for unethical practices. Four areas of concern are _____

_____

_____

25. Many businesses accept eight ethical g __ __ __ __ __ __ __ __ __. List them. _____

_____

_____

_____

_____

26. There are seven q __ __ __ __ __ __ __ __ that you can ask yourself when you must make an ethical decision. List them. _____

_____

_____

_____

● Your Career in Hospitality

Kick Off!

Activity A Name _____

Chapter 22 Date _____ Period _____

Part 1

Read each statement below. Write *yes* or *no* in the *Agree?* column. Be ready to explain your reasons for each answer.

Statement	Agree?	Text Supports?
1. Hospitality careers have more challenges than advantages.		
2. Learning about the hospitality industry and hospitality careers can help you determine if a hospitality career is for you.		
3. There is no way to find out what it is like to actually work in the hospitality industry.		
4. The Occupational Outlook Handbook is like a map that you can use to guide you to your career goal.		
5. Many jobs in hospitality require additional education or experience or both.		
6. Each higher level of the career ladder usually involves less responsibility and less stress, but usually higher pay.		

(continued)

Statement	Agree?	Text Supports?
7. Sources of education after high school include community colleges, business and career colleges, professional career schools, four-year colleges, and universities.		
8. Once you finish school, there is nothing more to learn.		
9. You can choose a career for yourself without thinking about your interests, aptitudes, abilities, or values.		
10. A career plan is not needed in the hospitality industry; you can just rise to the top.		

Part 2

Look in the text to find support for each statement. If the text supports a statement, write *yes* in the *Text Supports?* column. Then write the text page number in the space below the statement. If the text does not support the statement, write *no* in the *Text Supports?* column. Then, in the space below the statement, rewrite the statement so that it is supported by the text.

Hospitality Terms Chapter 22

Activity B

Chapter 22

Name _____

Date _____ Period _____

For each term in this chapter, develop a term overview. The term overview consists of three parts: a. your own definition, b. the textbook definition, and c. a sentence using the term. The first one is done for you.

1. stress

    a. Define the term in your own words.

    Tight muscles, tension, fear of an exam.

    b. Write the definition from the textbook.

    A feeling of tension that sometimes results from having too much to do, lack of time, difficult tasks, dangerous tasks, or unpredictable tasks.

    c. Write a sentence using the term.

    I was feeling a lot of stress because the exam was the same day as my brother's wedding.

2. information interview

    a. Define the term in your own words.

    _____

    _____

    b. Write the definition from the textbook.

    _____

    _____

    c. Write a sentence using the term.

    _____

    _____

3. job shadowing

    a. Define the term in your own words.

    _____

    _____

    b. Write the definition from the textbook.

    _____

    _____

    c. Write a sentence using the term.

    _____

    _____

(continued)

4. entry-level job

   a. Define the term in your own words.

_____

_____

   b. Write the definition from the textbook.

_____

_____

   c. Write a sentence using the term.

_____

_____

5. career ladder

   a. Define the term in your own words.

_____

_____

   b. Write the definition from the textbook.

_____

_____

   c. Write a sentence using the term.

_____

_____

6. postsecondary

   a. Define the term in your own words.

_____

_____

   b. Write the definition from the textbook.

_____

_____

   c. Write a sentence using the term.

_____

_____

7. internship

   a. Define the term in your own words.

_____

_____

(continued)

   b. Write the definition from the textbook.

   _____

   _____

   c. Write a sentence using the term.

   _____

   _____

8. apprenticeship

   a. Define the term in your own words.

   _____

   _____

   b. Write the definition from the textbook.

   _____

   _____

   c. Write a sentence using the term.

   _____

   _____

9. continuing professional education

   a. Define the term in your own words.

   _____

   _____

   b. Write the definition from the textbook.

   _____

   _____

   c. Write a sentence using the term.

   _____

   _____

10. aptitude

   a. Define the term in your own words.

   _____

   _____

   b. Write the definition from the textbook.

   _____

   _____

(continued)

c. Write a sentence using the term.

_____

_____

11. ability

    a. Define the term in your own words.

_____

_____

    b. Write the definition from the textbook.

_____

_____

    c. Write a sentence using the term.

_____

_____

12. career goal

    a. Define the term in your own words.

_____

_____

    b. Write the definition from the textbook.

_____

_____

    c. Write a sentence using the term.

_____

_____

13. career plan

    a. Define the term in your own words.

_____

_____

    b. Write the definition from the textbook.

_____

_____

    c. Write a sentence using the term.

_____

_____

Your Career in Hospitality

Activity C

Name _____

Chapter 22

Date _____ Period _____

Read each piece of advice below as if it has just been given to you by a group of hospitality workers. Which would be good advice for you to follow? Write **GA** in the blank for each piece of good advice. Write **BA** for each piece of bad advice. Then in the space provided, explain in your own words why the advice is good or bad.

_____ 1. Choose a career in hospitality if you want to work with diverse people.

_____

_____

_____ 2. You can find many opportunities for advancement in the hospitality industry.

_____

_____

_____ 3. Most jobs in the hospitality industry are desk jobs in which you will sit much of the time.

_____

_____

_____ 4. Of all hospitality jobs, restaurant work is the most likely to provide you with travel opportunities.

_____

_____

_____ 5. Hospitality jobs often have flexible working hours, which makes it easier to schedule work around family or school obligations.

_____

_____

_____ 6. Stress is a problem for all hospitality workers, and it prevents them from doing their best work.

_____

_____

_____ 7. Advancement in many hospitality careers often requires moving to another location.

_____

_____

_____ 8. There's no need to consider the occupational outlook for the career field you select.

_____

_____

(continued)

_____ 9. Job shadowing allows you to follow a person at work and learn whether you would enjoy his or her job.

_____

_____

_____ 10. Work experience in a job will allow you to decide if it is something you like enough to make a career of it.

_____

_____

_____ 11. The *Occupational Outlook Handbook* is a great resource to use in learning about careers.

_____

_____

_____ 12. Even if you are overqualified, it pays to take an entry-level job in order to advance into the career of your dreams.

_____

_____

_____ 13. Each higher level of the career ladder usually involves more responsibility, more money, and less stress.

_____

_____

_____ 14. Many jobs are available in the hospitality industry to a person without a high school diploma.

_____

_____

_____ 15. For students still in high school, tech prep programs or cooperative education programs offer good opportunities for training and work.

_____

_____

_____ 16. For students who do not want a four-year college degree, several options are available, including technical programs, community colleges, and professional career schools.

_____

_____

_____ 17. Classroom instruction is the only way to earn a four-year college degree.

_____

_____

(continued)

_____ 18. How well you know yourself and whether you like to work with people, things, or data is unimportant to your career.

_____

_____

_____ 19. Aptitude and ability will make a difference in whether you are happy in a job.

_____

_____

_____ 20. A career plan maps out how you plan to reach your career goal. It will help you get where you want to go.

_____

_____

Revisiting Chapter 22

Name _____

Date _____ Period _____

Write complete responses to the following questions and statements in the space provided.

1. List six advantages of working in the hospitality industry. _____

   _____

   _____

   _____

   _____

   _____

   _____

2. What are two factors that determine salaries and wages in the hospitality industry? _____

   _____

   _____

3. What are two factors that will determine whether a person advances in his or her career?_____

   _____

   _____

4. List four things that can be very challenging to workers in hospitality. _____

   _____

   _____

   _____

   _____

5. List four steps to take in deciding whether a career in hospitality is right for you. _____

   _____

   _____

   _____

   _____

6. Give five questions you might ask in an information interview about a career in which you are interested. _____

   _____

   _____

   _____

   _____

   _____

(continued)

7. What is an advantage to participating in a part-time, summer, or co-op job during high school?

_____

_____

_____

8. List five of the sections found in the *Occupational Outlook Handbook.* _____

_____

_____

_____

_____

_____

9. If you are interested in a hospitality career not listed in detail in the *Occupational Outlook Handbook,* in what section might you look? _____

_____

10. List five offerings of professional associations that may interest students considering jobs in the hospitality field._____

_____

_____

_____

_____

_____

11. Describe a career ladder._____

_____

_____

12. Compare cooperative education with tech prep. _____

_____

_____

_____

_____

13. What two college bachelor's degree majors are good options for students who want management careers in hospitality? _____

_____

_____

(continued)

14. How does a college certificate program differ from a college degree?_____
_____
_____
_____

15. List five ways to get continuing professional education for the hospitality industry. _____
_____
_____
_____
_____
_____

16. List the three steps in making a career decision. _____
_____
_____
_____

17. Describe the differences among jobs focusing on people, things, and data. Give an example of
each. _____
_____
_____
_____
_____
_____
_____

18. Compare aptitude and ability. _____
_____
_____
_____

19. Why is a career goal needed in order to develop a career plan? _____
_____
_____

20. Why is a career plan never final? _____
_____
_____

Skills for Success

Kick Off!

Activity A

Chapter 23

Name _____

Date _____ Period _____

Part 1

Read each statement below. Write *yes* or *no* in the *Agree?* column. Be ready to explain your reasons for each answer.

Statement	Agree?	Text Supports?
1. Deciding what career you will pursue is probably one of the biggest decisions you will ever make.		
2. Studying the career clusters is one of the best ways to learn about a variety of career options.		
3. Your choice of words has little or no effect on the customer.		
4. Nonverbal communication can change the meaning of words.		
5. Because hospitality is a people business, you don't need to know arithmetic or math.		
6. Three key job search skills are how to find job leads, how to fill out an application, and how to behave at an interview.		

(continued)

Statement	Agree?	Text Supports?
7. Once you get a job, you don't have to worry about how you look or your attitude.		
8. While you are climbing the career ladder, you can neglect your health.		
9. Four active steps in advancing in your career include continuing education, developing leadership skills, being active in professional organizations, and changing jobs.		
10. When you make a career decision, you do not need to consider how your career will affect other roles you plan to have.		

Part 2

Look in the text to find support for each statement. If the text supports a statement, write *yes* in the *Text Supports?* column. Then write the text page number in the space below the statement. If the text does not support the statement, write *no* in the *Text Supports?* column. Then, in the space below the statement, rewrite the statement so that it is supported by the text.

Hospitality Terms Chapter 23

Activity B

Chapter 23

Name _____

Date _____ Period _____

Part 1

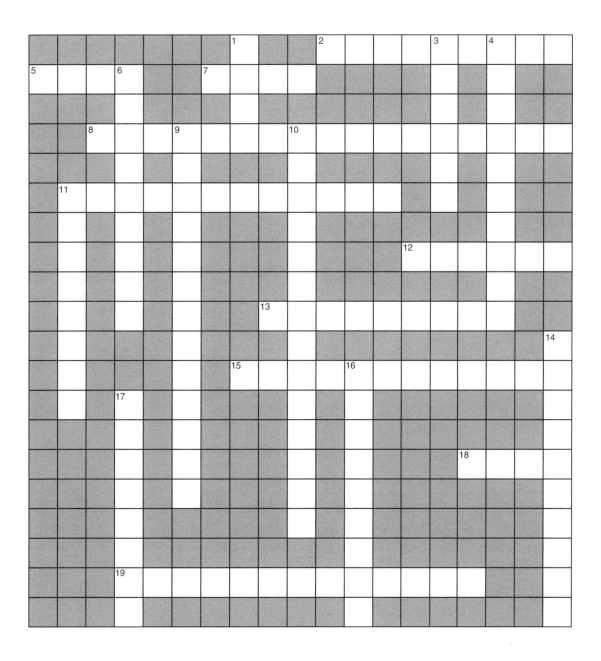

(continued)

Across

2. A formal meeting between two or more people during which questions are asked of one person.

5. A job _____ is information that directs you toward a job opening.

7. Nonverbal communication that includes facial expressions, posture, hand gestures, and tone of voice is called _____ language.

8. Proper behavior for a business situation is known as _____ _____.

11. The ability to make changes to match new situations.

12. The basic, routine actions you carry out every day at work are work _____.

13. Proper behavior in social situations, also known as manners.

15. Notifying your supervisor that you intend to leave your job is called _____ _____.

18. A _____ letter is written by a job applicant to introduce him or her, highlight his or her strengths, and ask for an interview.

19. The transmission of information and feelings from one person to another.

Down

1. A set of responsibilities and expectations that go with an aspect of your life.

3. A written document that lists a person's qualifications for a job, including education and work experience.

4. Ability to get a job done on your own without someone constantly reminding you.

6. A deliberate use of a substance in ways that harm health is known as _____ _____.

9. _____ skills consist of the ability to interact smoothly and productively with other people.

10. The inner urge to achieve your goals is known as _____-_____.

11. The way you look at the world and the way you respond to things that happen.

14. The ability to influence others and to inspire excellence.

16. _____ communication conveys information and feelings without using words.

17. The process of resolving a disagreement in a peaceful way is known as _____ resolution.

(continued)

Part 2

One way to learn about a term is to analyze it for words or word parts that you already know. You will develop a term analysis for each term below. The term analysis has four parts: a. list of the words or parts of words in the term that you recognize, b. list of other terms that contain one or more of the words or word parts, c. definition based on this analysis, and d. the definition from the textbook.

1. electronic communication

    a. Write the words or word parts that you recognize.

    _____

    b. Write other terms you know that contain these words or word parts.

    _____

    c. Write a definition based on your analysis of the words and word parts.

    _____

    _____

    d. Write the definition from the textbook.

    _____

    _____

2. negotiation

    a. Write the words or word parts that you recognize.

    _____

    b. Write other terms you know that contain these words or word parts.

    _____

    c. Write a definition based on your analysis of the words and word parts.

    _____

    _____

    d. Write the definition from the textbook.

    _____

3. cooperation

    a. Write the words or word parts that you recognize.

    _____

    b. Write other terms you know that contain these words or word parts.

    _____

(continued)

c. Write a definition based on your analysis of the words and word parts.

_____

_____

d. Write the definition from the textbook.

_____

_____

4. reference

a. Write the words or word parts that you recognize.

_____

b. Write other terms you know that contain these words or word parts.

_____

c. Write a definition based on your analysis of the words and word parts.

_____

_____

d. Write the definition from the textbook.

_____

_____

Skills for Success

Name _____

Date _____ Period _____

Write complete answers to each of the following questions or statements in the space provided.

1. List the four career pathways included in the hospitality and tourism career cluster. _____

_____

_____

_____

_____

2. Describe how nonverbal communication can give two different meanings to the phrase, "Welcome to the Bluebird Bed-and-Breakfast." _____

_____

_____

_____

_____

3. Describe good listening skills. _____

_____

_____

_____

4. How do conflict resolution and negotiation differ? _____

_____

_____

_____

_____

5. List four places where job leads can be found. _____

_____

_____

_____

6. Compare the content of a resume to the content of a cover letter. _____

_____

_____

_____

7. What should you include in a thank-you letter following an interview? _____

_____

_____

(continued)

8. Why is grooming so important on the job? _____

_____

_____

9. List four components of a positive attitude. _____

_____

_____

10. Reno and Maria both work as front desk agents at a hotel. The hotel has purchased a new computer program and is requiring employees to be trained to use it. Reno complains constantly, telling Maria why he doesn't think it will work. He says the old program was good enough, and the new program will just confuse him and the customers. Which of the four components of a positive attitude does Reno need to work on, and why? _____

_____

_____

11. Jewel has applied for a job as assistant manager of a small hotel. She very much wants the position. As part of the interview process, she is taken to dinner at a fine restaurant. What are some points of etiquette for which her interviewers might be observing her? _____

_____

_____

_____

12. Tyson has just graduated from college and is starting a job as a trainee for the night manager position at a restaurant. Because Tyson has never worked nights before, he is concerned about his health. What advice would you give Tyson? _____

_____

_____

_____

13. Steven has worked as a server in the same fine-dining restaurant for over 10 years. He recently married and has decided he wants to make more money. Steven thinks he might advance by working as the assistant manager and then the manager. Because he has never had this goal before, he has not done much to prepare for it. What would you suggest that Steven do now so he will be ready to apply for an assistant manager position by the end of the year? _____

_____

_____

_____

_____

14. List all the roles you expect to have 10 years from now. _____

_____

_____

_____

Hospitality and Tourism Career Cluster

Activity D

Name _____

Chapter 23

Date _____ Period _____

The four career pathways included in the hospitality and tourism career cluster are listed below. Place a check in front of two career pathways that interest you.

_____ Restaurants and food and beverage services

_____ Lodging

_____ Travel and tourism

_____ Recreation, amusements, and attractions

In the space below, indicate the career pathways you checked and list four occupations for each pathway. Explain your interest in each occupation.

Name of career pathway: _____

Occupations: Reasons for your interest:

1. _____   _____

2. _____   _____

3. _____   _____

4. _____   _____

Name of career pathway: _____

Occupations: Reasons for your interest:

1. _____   _____

2. _____   _____

3. _____   _____

4. _____   _____

From all the occupations you listed, identify the two that interest you most.

Occupation 1: _____

Occupation 2: _____

List the abilities and skills needed for the occupations listed above.

Occupation 1: _____

_____

Occupation 2: _____

_____

Do you have the abilities and skills listed? What can you do to develop any abilities and skills you do not have? _____

_____

_____

Revisiting Chapter 23

Name _____

Date _____ Period _____

Read the following statements about skills for career success. If the statement is true, write *T* in the blank. If the statement is false, rewrite the underlined portion of the statement to make it true.

_____ 1. Each individual decides how to use his or her <u>unique skills and abilities.</u>

_____

_____ 2. Workplace skills <u>include job search skills, work habits, attitudes, maintaining physical and mental health, and learning how to balance multiple roles.</u>

_____

_____

_____ 3. The career clusters are <u>10</u> groups of occupational and career specialities.

_____

_____ 4. The occupations in each career clusters pathway range from <u>entry-level positions to advanced positions.</u>

_____

_____ 5. Communication includes the words you choose and <u>your body language.</u>

_____

_____ 6. Listening and speaking are the <u>most advanced</u> forms of communication.

_____

_____ 7. <u>Skillful conflict resolution</u> requires communication skills and interpersonal skills.

_____

_____ 8. A person needs to <u>understand numbers and mathematics</u> in order to use a calculator and computer properly.

_____

_____ 9. The ability to use electronic communication tools <u>is not essential</u> for today's successful businessperson.

_____

_____ 10. Business e-mail <u>should never include</u> abbreviations and emoticons.

_____

_____ 11. Job applications are <u>seldom available</u> by just walking into a business such as a chain restaurant.

_____

_____ 12. Online job applications <u>need to be printed off and mailed.</u>

(continued)

_____ 12. Online job applications <u>need to be printed off and mailed</u>.

_____

_____ 13. The best people to use as references are <u>relatives, such as your parents</u>.

_____

_____ 14. A <u>job interview</u> is a way for the employer to learn about the job applicant and decide whether to offer him or her the job.

_____

_____ 15. A good handshake is firm, <u>lasts about 10 seconds</u>, and is done with the right hand.

_____

_____ 16. During an interview, it is good practice to <u>say negative things about yourself and previous employers</u>.

_____

_____

_____ 17. The interview is a time when it is appropriate for <u>both the interviewer and the interviewee</u> to ask questions.

_____

_____ 18. You may <u>expect to take a test</u> when you interview for many types of jobs.

_____

_____ 19. People who work in <u>foodservice</u> have specific sanitation-related grooming and dress requirements.

_____

_____ 20. Business etiquette is <u>universal, or the same around the world</u>.

_____

_____ 21. <u>All employers</u> will pay for college classes or professional training, especially if it is related to your job.

_____

_____ 22. <u>Volunteering to lead projects</u> at work is a good way to develop leadership skills.

_____

_____ 23. Participation and involvement <u>in a professional association</u> is one of the main ways to keep up-to-date in your profession.

_____

_____ 24. When you are looking for a job with another company, you should use <u>work time</u> to submit your resume and interview.

_____

_____ 25. One of the challenges of life is to <u>balance the many roles</u> you have as they compete for your time.

_____

● Starting a Business

Kick Off!

Activity A

Chapter 24

Name _____

Date _____ Period _____

Part 1

Read each statement below. Write *yes* or *no* in the *Agree?* column. Be ready to explain your reasons for each answer.

Statement	Agree?	Text Supports?
1. All great businesses in the United States were started by entrepreneurs.		
2. Most entrepreneurs started their businesses because their parents pushed them.		
3. There are three ways to start a new business: buy an existing business, buy a franchise, and start from scratch.		
4. Many businesses are sold because they are not making a profit.		
5. The franchisee must follow the rules set by the franchisor.		
6. The three forms of business ownership are sole proprietorship, partnership, and corporation.		

(continued)

Statement	Agree?	Text Supports?
7. You don't need much money to start a new business.		
8. In order to get a loan for a new business, most banks require a business plan.		
9. The parts of a business plan include executive summary, description of business, industry/market analysis, customers, marketing plan, operations plan, financial plan, and growth plan.		
10. The U.S. Small Business Administration (SBA) is the main government agency that helps new businesses and entrepreneurs.		

Part 2

Look in the text to find support for each statement. If the text supports a statement, write *yes* in the *Text Supports?* column. Then write the text page number in the space below the statement. If the text does not support the statement, write *no* in the *Text Supports?* column. Then, in the space below the statement, rewrite the statement so that it is supported by the text.

Hospitality Terms Chapter 24

Name _____

Date _____ Period _____

Part 1

Before looking at the chapter, think about words you have heard or used in connection to starting a business. List them.

_____   _____

_____   _____

_____   _____

_____   _____

Part 2

Compare your list of words to the "Terms to Know" list for Chapter 24. Write any words in the "Terms to Know" list that were not in your list.

_____   _____

_____   _____

_____   _____

_____

Part 3

For each of the following terms, first write the definition from the textbook. Then write a sentence using the term in context.

1. entrepreneurship _____

_____

_____

_____

_____

(continued)

2. entrepreneur _____

_____

_____

_____

_____

3. franchise fee _____

_____

_____

_____

_____

4. loan _____

_____

_____

_____

_____

5. business plan _____

_____

_____

_____

_____

6. start-up costs _____

_____

_____

_____

_____

7. U.S. Small Business Administration _____

_____

_____

_____

_____

8. chamber of commerce _____

_____

_____

_____

_____

Becoming an Entrepreneur

Activity C

Chapter 24

Name _____

Date _____ Period _____

Part 1

Nathan and Maria ask your advice on what to do to start their own business. In Column A, list the three basic ways to start a new business. Use Column B to describe the advantages of each and Column C to describe the disadvantages of each way.

A. Options	B. Advantages	C. Disadvantages
1.		
2.		
3.		

Part 2

1. Nathan and Maria have a great idea for starting a new business, but they do not have enough money for start-up costs. They have been considering a loan. What would you recommend as two of the most likely possible sources of business loans? _____

   _____

   _____

2. They have heard that special funds are often available to minority entrepreneurs. They wonder if this might help them start their business. What is the name of the government agency they could contact about these funds? _____

   _____

(continued)

Part 3

Nathan and Maria are preparing to write a business plan, which they will submit as a part of their loan application. In Column A, list the eight parts of a business plan. In Column B, describe the purpose of each part.

A. Parts of the plan	B. Purpose
1.	
2.	
3.	
4.	
5.	
6.	
7.	
8.	

(continued)

Part 4

Nathan and Maria want to know what resources that small business entrepreneurs can use to gather information and to assist them in creating a business plan. In Column A, list four resources available in every state. In Column B, describe the type of help that each resource can provide.

A. Resource	B. Type of help available
1.	
2.	
3.	
4.	

Entrepreneurship Scramble

Name _____

Date _____ Period _____

Unscramble the letters in the following phrases. Use the terms to compose a story about someone wanting to start a hospitality business. Then, circle the terms in your story.

_____ 1. erntureepren

_____ 2. ttras-pu sscot

_____ 3. sssneiub lpna

_____ 4. S.U. lmaSl isuBsnse naAdonimiisttr

_____ 5. hmabrec fo rceemocm

_____ 6. rfncaesih efe

_____ 7. preertsneruenpih

_____ 8. nloa

Once upon a time, _____

_____

_____

_____

_____

_____

_____

_____

_____

_____

_____

_____

_____

_____

_____

_____

_____

_____

_____

_____

Revisiting Chapter 24

Activity E   Name _____

Chapter 24   Date _____ Period _____

Write complete responses to the following questions and statements in the space provided.

1. List the eight characteristics of a successful entrepreneur. _____

   _____

   _____

   _____

   _____

2. Under what heading of the newspaper classified ads would you likely find listings for businesses to buy? _____

   _____

3. Name one advantage of buying an existing business. _____

   _____

   _____

4. What is the main disadvantage of buying an existing business? _____

   _____

   _____

5. Give one advantage of buying a franchise. _____

   _____

   _____

6. Name one disadvantage of buying a franchise. _____

   _____

   _____

7. Give one advantage of starting a business from scratch. _____

   _____

   _____

8. Name one disadvantage of starting a business from scratch. _____

   _____

   _____

9. List the three business ownership structures. _____

   _____

   _____

(continued)

_____

10. What are four things an entrepreneur will need to be able to pay for before the business starts to earn money? _____

_____

_____

11. Describe a loan. _____

_____

12. What two things does an entrepreneur have to do in order to obtain a loan? _____

_____

_____

13. Which part of a business plan is the last part to be written, and why? _____

_____

_____

14. What three things should be included in the description of the business? _____

_____

_____

_____

15. List four things that need to go into the industry/market analysis of a business plan. _____

_____

_____

_____

16. What section of the business plan discusses the day-to-day operations of the business? _____

_____

17. What does the financial plan describe? _____

_____

_____

18. Describe the purpose of the U.S. Small Business Administration. _____

_____

_____

19. What does the acronym *SCORE* stand for, and what does this group do? _____

_____

_____

_____

20. What are three things that chambers of commerce may offer to assist new entrepreneurs? _____

_____

_____

_____